The Critical Idiom
General Editor: JOHN D. JUMP

---

22   Burlesque

In the same series

Burlesque/*John D. Jump*

Methuen & Co Ltd

First published 1972
by Methuen & Co Ltd
11 New Fetter Lane, London EC4
© John D. Jump
Printed in Great Britain
by Cox & Wyman Ltd, Fakenham, Norfolk

SBN 416 66650 7 Hardback
SBN 416 66660 4 Paperback

Distributed in the U.S.A.
by Barnes & Noble Inc.

To LUCY, MATTHEW,
POLLY, *and* TOBY

Contents

Preface

This volume is one of a series of short studies, each dealing with a single key item, or a group of two or three key items, in our critical vocabulary. The purpose of the series differs from that served by the standard glossaries of literary terms. Many terms are adequately defined for the needs of students by the brief entries in these glossaries, and such terms are not the subjects of studies in the present series. But there are other terms which cannot be made familiar by means of compact definitions. Students need to grow accustomed to them through simple and straightforward but reasonably full discussions of them. The purpose of this series is to provide such discussions.

Some of the terms in question refer to literary movements (e.g., 'Romanticism', 'Aestheticism', etc.), others to literary kinds (e.g., 'Comedy', 'The Epic', etc.), and still others to stylistic features (e.g., 'Irony', 'The Conceit', etc.). Because of this diversity of subject-matter, no attempt has been made to impose a uniform pattern upon the studies. But all authors have tried to provide as full illustrative quotation as possible, to make reference whenever appropriate to more than one literature, and to compose their studies in such a way as to guide readers towards the short bibliographies in which they have made suggestions for further reading.

In the present volume I have adopted a sharp and simple definition of 'burlesque' and I have tried to distinguish clearly between the different forms that burlesque can take. I have introduced a large number of examples. Some of these, by refusing to fit neatly into single categories, provide useful reminders that my definitions must not be pressed too hard. But I believe that collectively they demonstrate the general validity of my distinctions.

I owe much to the friends who have from time to time discussed with me the matters treated in this book. My colleague Dr A. J. N. Wilson kindly read and commented upon the complete typescript. Members of the *Critical Quarterly* Society gave an encouraging reception to the chapter on Parody which I delivered as a lecture at their 1971 conference in Winchester. My wife read and criticized early drafts of some of the parts as well as the final draft of the whole. Miss Diane Cansdale prepared the typescript with speed and efficiency.

For permission to quote from works still in copyright, I make grateful acknowledgement as follows:

Ancient Music by Ezra Pound is reprinted by permission of Faber & Faber Ltd from *Collected Shorter Poems*; and by permission of New Directions Publishing Corporation of New York, from *Personae* (© Ezra Pound, 1926).

The lines from *The Guerdon* by Max Beerbohm are reprinted from *A Variety of Things* by permission of William Heinemann Ltd; and Alfred A. Knopf Inc of New York.

The lines from *Scruts* by Max Beerbohm are reprinted from *A Christmas Garland* by permission of William Heinemann Ltd; and E. P. Dutton & Co Inc of New York.

The quotations from poems by Cecil Day Lewis are reprinted from *Collected Poems* 1954 by permission of Messrs. Jonathan Cape Ltd and The Hogarth Press Ltd; and by permission of the Harold Matson Company Inc of New York (© C. Day Lewis).

The lines from Henry Reed's *Chard Whitlow* are reprinted by permission of Messrs Jonathan Cape Ltd.

J. D. Jump

University of Manchester

I

Definitions

For many Americans today, a burlesque is a kind of variety show with a heavy emphasis upon sex, featuring broad comedians and strip-tease dancers. This is not the sense that concerns us here. For more than three centuries English-speaking literary critics have been using the word in a sense that Richmond P. Bond admirably defines. 'Burlesque consists,' he writes, 'in the use or imitation of serious matter or manner, made amusing by the creation of an incongruity between style and subject' (*English Burlesque Poetry 1700–1750*, p. 3). Examples of such incongruous use or imitation include Beaumont's *Knight of the Burning Pestle*, Butler's *Hudibras*, Pope's *Rape of the Lock*, Fielding's *Shamela* and *Joseph Andrews*, and Byron's *Vision of Judgment*.

These represent several different species of burlesque. One line of distinction among them would separate those in which a relatively trifling subject is ludicrously elevated by the style of presentation from those in which a relatively important subject is ludicrously degraded by the style of presentation. *The Rape of the Lock* and *Shamela* would fall on one side of this line as instances of the high burlesque, and *Hudibras* and *The Vision of Judgment* on the other as instances of the low burlesque. Another line would divide those which burlesque particular originals from those which burlesque something more general. *Shamela* and *The Vision of Judgment* imitate and ridicule particular works by Richardson and Southey respectively; *The Rape of the Lock* mocks the epic in general, and *Hudibras* degrades the lofty pretensions of Puritanism.

These two intersecting lines of demarcation give us four species of burlesque:

1. Travesty, the low burlesque of a particular work achieved by treating the subject of that work in an aggressively familiar style: e.g., Byron's *Vision of Judgment*.
2. Hudibrastic, the low burlesque of a less confined material: e.g., Butler's *Hudibras*.
3. Parody, the high burlesque of a particular work (or author) achieved by applying the style of that work (or author) to a less worthy subject: e.g., Fielding's *Shamela*.
4. The Mock-Poem, commonly the mock-epic, the high burlesque of a whole class of literature achieved by lavishing the style characteristic of the class upon a trifling subject: e.g., Pope's *Rape of the Lock*.

Historically, the low burlesque prevailed in the seventeenth century, travesty and Hudibrastic flourishing vigorously during the Restoration period. The high burlesque came into its own in the eighteenth century, which saw the composition of most of our finest mock-epic or mock-heroic works. There was great activity in parody, too, and this persisted throughout the nineteenth century and into the twentieth century. We must not over-simplify, however; each of these periods can show examples of all four species of burlesque. Examples occur in earlier periods, too. But concentration upon post-medieval examples, and in the main upon examples in English, seems prudent in a study as brief as the present.

After a discussion of each of the species in turn, I shall devote a separate chapter to dramatic burlesques. These represent so well-established a tradition in the English theatre that dividing them among the species and considering them apart from one another would obscure a good deal of their interest.

2

Travesty

Travesty enjoyed a great vogue in seventeenth-century France, the *Virgile travesti* (from 1648) of Paul Scarron being the most famous example of the species. The fashion quickly spread to England, where it flourished during the Restoration period and into the eighteenth century. Admittedly, there had been English travesties of earlier date: for example, the puppet-show in Ben Jonson's *Bartholomew Fair* (1614). But the French influence, and above all that of Scarron, caused a rapid increase in the production of familiar and irreverent renderings of works by Virgil, Homer, Ovid, and other respected authors.

One of the most genial of these is Swift's 'Baucis and Philemon' (1709), which burlesques a story told in the eighth book of Ovid's *Metamorphoses*. According to Ovid, Baucis and Philemon, an elderly Phrygian couple, show hospitality to Jove and Hermes without recognizing their guests. In gratitude, the gods transform their humble cottage into a temple and ask what more they can do for them.

> A while they whisper; then to *Jove* address'd,
> *Philemon* thus prefers their joint Request.
> We crave to serve before your sacred Shrine,
> And offer at your Altars Rites Divine:
> And since not any Action of our Life
> Has been polluted with Domestick Strife,
> We beg one Hour of Death; that neither she
> With Widows Tears may live to bury me,
> Nor weeping I, with wither'd Arms may bear
> My breathless *Baucis* to the Sepulcher.

> (tr. Dryden)

The gods grant these requests and Baucis and Philemon at the end of their days are metamorphosed into two trees.

Swift retains the names Baucis and Philemon but turns the pagan gods into Christian saints and locates the action in Kent. The saints transform the cottage into an English parish church; and, when they ask the couple what more they can do for them,

> *Philemon*, having paus'd awhile,
> Return'd 'em Thanks in homely Style;
> Then said, My House is grown so fine,
> Methinks I still would call it mine:
> I'm old, and fain would live at Ease,
> Make me the *Parson*, if you please.
>
> He spoke, and presently he feels
> His Grazier's Coat fall down his Heels;
> He sees, yet hardly can believe,
> About each Arm a Pudding-sleeve;
> His Wastcoat to a Cassock grew,
> And both assum'd a sable Hue;
> But being Old, continu'd just
> As Thread-bare, and as full of Dust.
> His Talk was now of *Tythes* and *Dues*;
> He smok'd his Pipe, and read the News;
> Knew how to preach old Sermons next,
> Vamp'd in the Preface and the Text;
> At Christ'nings well could act his Part,
> And had the Service all by Heart;
> Wish'd Women might have Children fast,
> And thought whose Sow had farrow'd last:
> Against *Dissenters* would repine,
> And stood up firm for *Right Divine*:
> Found his Head fill'd with many a System,
> But Classick Authors, – he ne'er miss'd 'em.

Swift elaborates each of the transformations in this fanciful way. When the cottage becomes a church, its chimney becomes the steeple, its kettle the bell, its jack (for turning the spit) the clock, a chair the pulpit, the bedstead the pews, and so on. Everything is so thoroughly naturalized and familiarized that Swift can even permit himself a little good-humoured satire at the expense of Philemon as representing the Anglican clergy. From beginning to end, his style is simple, easy, and informal.

Perhaps an even finer travesty, and certainly a more savage one, is *The Vision of Judgment* (1822) by Byron. This differs from the travesties mentioned so far in that it relates not to any of the works of classical antiquity but to a poem by one of its author's contemporaries. It burlesques *A Vision of Judgement* (1821) by Southey.

In 1820, George III had died, old, mad, and blind, after a reign of sixty years. As Poet Laureate, Southey felt it incumbent upon himself to celebrate the reception of the deceased monarch into celestial bliss, and as a convert to Toryism he was the readier to do so because he approved of the policies of the late King's governments. *A Vision of Judgement* tells how the King awakens after death and raises his eyes heavenward. The spirit of a Tory Prime Minister who had been killed about the time the King went permanently insane notifies him of the firmness and wisdom with which the Prince Regent has been ruling in his place and of the defeat of Napoleon. He confesses that, despite this triumph, the spirit of Jacobinism, or subversive Liberalism, remains dreadfully active. The King progresses to the gate of heaven, where he is to be judged. Invited to 'bring forth his accusers', the Fiend responsible for the revolutions which had troubled the reign just ended produces John Wilkes the agitator and 'Junius' the political journalist. But even they lack the effrontery to accuse so blameless a monarch, and the Fiend hurls them back into hell. Some of those who had wronged George III in life are now ready to admit their fault, and George Washington is prominent among these. The beatification of the King and his welcome into heaven by his predecessors on the throne, by the great men of the past, and by those members of his family whom he had outlived, complete Southey's poem.

Southey writes in unrhymed accentual hexameters and with a deliberate assumption of dignity. But his hexameters limp and drag; his Miltonic vagueness cannot obscure the absurdity of his identification of the heavenly host with the Tory party; his writing is flat, and his tone is merely pompous.

Byron thought *A Vision of Judgement* a presumptuous poem because it told God what he ought to do with George III; he detested it as a Tory poem, the work of one whom he considered a bigoted renegade; and he knew it to be a bad poem, inflated, tame, stilted, and preposterous. A travesty covering very much the same ground in an aggressively familiar style seemed the obvious corrective.

He did not take over Southey's metrical form any more than Scarron took over Virgil's. He relied upon the octave stanza, *ottava rima*, which long practice in *Don Juan* had made second nature to him. This allows him to 'rattle on exactly as I'd talk/With any body in a ride or walk' (*Don Juan*, XV. xix). Thrown off in this casual tone, his more outrageous utterances invariably take his readers by surprise.

He sets his poem where much of Southey's is set, just outside the gate of heaven; but instead of aspiring to a Miltonic dignity and generality he renders his setting and characters in the most familiar and prosaic of particular terms:

> Saint Peter sat by the celestial gate:
> His keys were rusty, and the lock was dull ...   (i)

Business is so slack that Peter nods over his keys and has to be wakened by a cherub who 'flapped his right wing o'er his eyes' (xvii). A cantankerous janitor, he recalls that he had impetuously used force in an attempt to exclude the guillotined Louis XVI from unmerited bliss and reminds us that in life he had cut off the right ear of Malchus, the high priest's servant, in an attempt to rescue Jesus (John xviii. 10). We are not surprised when he protests, as the first pope, against the beatification of such an enemy of Catholic Emancipation as George III. He is a snob, too, in his attitude towards a belated convert: 'That fellow Paul – the parvenù!' (xx).

This buffoon evidently ranks lower in the social scale than the patricians Michael and Satan, the spokesmen of heaven and hell for the soul of the dead King. Michael patronizes him. Satan's hostile glance makes him sweat 'through his Apostolic skin' (xxv) and brings the cherubs to his rescue, 'for by many stories,/And true, we learn the Angels all are Tories' (xxvi). At Michael's invitation, Satan states his case for George's damnation.

He speaks with poise, acknowledging the King's domestic virtues and conceding that he acted as the tool of powerful political interests. Nevertheless, this tool had contributed to make his own reign as bloody as any in history and 'ever warred with freedom and the free' (xlv). Invited to call his witnesses, Satan produces a daunting multitude of them. After being taken aback for a moment, Michael collects himself and suggests a limitation to 'two honest, clean,/True testimonies' (lxiii). Satan accordingly summons the two who failed the Fiend in Southey's *Vision of Judgement*, John Wilkes and 'Junius'.

The stanzas introducing Wilkes form a conveniently compact illustration of the style in which Byron travesties Southey's poem. Wilkes, turbulent Radical, inveterate electioneer, cross-eyed womanizer, and jaunty wit, had enjoyed great notoriety half a century earlier. Southey has no difficulty in recognizing him:

> Beholding the foremost,
> Him by the cast of his eye oblique, I knew as the firebrand
> Whom the unthinking populace held for their idol and hero,
> Lord of Misrule in his day.

(v)

B

Byron gets rid of this solemnity. His Wilkes speaks in an extremely brisk and racy fashion. Michael's more grave and measured utterances – 'If you have aught to arraign in him, the tomb/Gives license', etc. – highlight the cheerful impudence of the politician who carries into eternity the electioneering habits of a lifetime:

> A merry, cock-eyed, curious-looking Sprite
>   Upon the instant started from the throng,
> Dressed in a fashion now forgotten quite;
>   For all the fashions of the flesh stick long
> By people in the next world; where unite
>   All the costumes since Adam's, right or wrong,
> From Eve's fig-leaf down to the petticoat,
> Almost as scanty, of days less remote.
>
> The Spirit looked around upon the crowds
>   Assembled, and exclaimed, 'My friends of all
> The spheres, we shall catch cold amongst these clouds;
>   So let's to business: why this general call?
> If those are freeholders I see in shrouds,
>   And 'tis for an election that they bawl,
> Behold a candidate with unturned coat!
> Saint Peter, may I count upon your vote?'
>
> 'Sir,' replied Michael, 'you mistake; these things
>   Are of a former life, and what we do
> Above is more august; to judge of kings
>   Is the tribunal met: so now you know.'
> 'Then I presume those gentlemen with wings,'
>   Said Wilkes, 'are Cherubs; and that soul below
> Looks much like George the Third, but to my mind
> A good deal older – bless me! is he blind?'
>
> 'He is what you behold him, and his doom
>   Depends upon his deeds,' the Angel said;
> 'If you have aught to arraign in him, the tomb
>   Gives license to the humblest beggar's head
> To lift itself against the loftiest.' – 'Some,'

Said Wilkes, 'don't wait to see them laid in lead,
For such a liberty – and I, for one,
Have told them what I thought beneath the sun.'

'*Above* the sun repeat, then, what thou hast
   To urge against him,' said the Archangel. 'Why,'
Replied the spirit, 'since old scores are past,
   Must I turn evidence? In faith, not I.
Besides, I beat him hollow at the last,
   With all his Lords and Commons: in the sky
I don't like ripping up old stories, since
His conduct was but natural in a prince.'

(lxvi–lxx)

Though Wilkes' lack of vindictiveness makes him useless to the
prosecution, 'Junius' is more helpful; and Satan is just suggesting
that further witnesses should be summoned, including George
Washington, when the devil Asmodeus interrupts the proceedings.
He carries in the poet Southey whom he has just apprehended in
the act of writing *A Vision of Judgement*. After some ludicrous
exchanges, Southey insists on reading his poem aloud.

This brings the proceeding to an abrupt close. There is a
general flight from the spot, and Peter knocks down the poet with
his keys. In the confusion, the feeble-minded old King slips
unnoticed into heaven,

And when the tumult dwindled to a calm,
I left him practising the hundredth psalm.

(cvi)

In this way, Byron avoids the presumptuousness that a deliberate
verdict on the King would have entailed. He concludes in a good-
humoured, even charitable, vein, without compromising the truth
about as bad a King as ever 'left a realm undone' (viii).

The twentieth century has seen a fashion in works that repeat in
contemporary terms the situations and characters occurring in
particular classical originals. Eugene O'Neill's *Mourning Becomes*

Electra and T. S. Eliot's *Cocktail Party* are among the most widely known of these. Since neither of them burlesques its original, neither approximates to travesty. But what about Joyce's *Ulysses* (1922)?

This novel of modern Dublin renders in a thoroughly unheroic manner a story paralleling that of the *Odyssey*. Homer's epic falls into three parts. Its first four books describe the predicament of Telemachus, the son of Odysseus (Ulysses), and his quest for his father. The wanderings of Odysseus, narrated largely in his own words, occupy slightly more than the next eight books. The last twelve books are almost entirely concerned with the homecoming of Odysseus, his massacre of the suitors who have tried to take advantage of his long absence, and his reunion with his faithful wife Penelope. Joyce likewise divides his novel into three parts. His first three episodes describe a morning spent by Stephen Dedalus, a young man who is alienated from his father. The next twelve trace a day's wanderings around Dublin by Leopold Bloom, a father who has lost a son. The two men get to know each other, and the last three episodes show us their arrival at Bloom's house, where Molly Bloom, unlike Penelope, has welcomed a lover during her husband's absence.

Joyce associates each of his eighteen episodes with an appropriate incident or character in the *Odyssey*. Thus, Leopold Bloom's attendance at a funeral in Glasnevin Cemetery links with Odysseus' evocation of the spirits of the dead; Bloom's visit to a newspaper office links with Odysseus' stay at the home of Aeolus, who had dominion over the winds; the irascible Sinn Feiner who attacks Bloom in Barney Kiernan's tavern links with the cannibalistic Cyclops into whose cave Odysseus rashly enters and from which he escapes with great difficulty; and Bella Cohen's brothel links with the island of Circe.

Only an insensitive reader could assume that the purpose of these associations is merely to contrast ancient heroism and poetry with modern meanness and prose. While we read, our attention is almost completely absorbed by the immediate affairs of Stephen Dedalus, Leopold and Molly Bloom, and the rest. We are hardly aware of the Homeric parallels. If and when we do notice them, they serve to enrich this modern subject-matter, so that we see the persons and their Dublin in an almost legendary light. Clearly *Ulysses* is no travesty, for we lose sight for long periods of the very material that would be the object of such a burlesque, and in any case we sense little incongruity between that material and the modern characters and incidents that dominate our minds.

Joyce's novel contains particular elements that will require consideration later. Its relevance here is that it makes a near approach to a species to which it does not in fact belong. By doing so, it complements the positive instances previously discussed in sharpening our conception of travesty.

3
Hudibrastic

Like travesty, Hudibrastic is a form of low burlesque. But, whereas travesty aims at a particular author or work, Hudibrastic has a wider target. The long poem from which it takes its name, Butler's *Hudibras* (from 1662), attacks the religious and political attitudes of the Puritans, who had held power during the period from the outbreak of the Civil War in 1642 to the Restoration of the monarchy in 1660. Incidentally, it derides the virtuosi of the newly chartered Royal Society.

Among the Puritans, Butler distinguishes between the Presbyterians, who for a time had led the opposition to the monarchy, and the Independents, who had displaced them when the rebellion gave birth to a military dictatorship. Hudibras, a knight of some education, is a Presbyterian; Ralpho, his squire, an ignorant tailor, is an Independent. Though both would be men of standing among their fellows, Butler regards them disparagingly, even jeeringly, and presents them in a deliberately casual, slapdash manner.

He mocks the scholastic learning and the pedantry of the knight. After reviewing his attainments in logic, rhetoric, mathematics and philosophy, Butler observes that

> He could raise Scruples dark and nice,
> And after solve 'em in a trice:
> As if Divinity had catch'd
> The Itch, of purpose to be scratch'd;
> Or, like a Mountebank, did wound
> And stab her self with doubts profound,
> Onely to shew with how small pain
> The sores of faith are cur'd again;

> Although by woful proof we find,
> They alwayes leave a Scar behind. (I. i. 161–70)

Though Hudibras himself exhibits no great valour, his party had shown itself only too ready to employ violence in the service of its wrongheaded beliefs.

> For his *Religion* it was fit
> To match his Learning and his Wit:
> 'Twas *Presbyterian* true blew,
> For he was of that stubborn Crew
> Of Errant Saints, whom all men grant
> To be the true Church *Militant*:
> Such as do build their Faith upon
> The holy Text of *Pike* and *Gun*;
> Decide all Controversies by
> Infallible *Artillery*;
> And prove their Doctrine Orthodox
> By Apostolick *Blows* and *Knocks*;
> Call Fire and Sword and Desolation,
> A *godly-thorough-Reformation*,
> Which alwayes must be carry'd on,
> And still be doing, never done:
> As if Religion were intended
> For nothing else but to be mended.
> A Sect, whose chief Devotion lies
> In odde perverse Antipathies;
> In falling out with that or this,
> And finding somewhat still amiss:
> More peevish, cross, and spleenatick,
> Then Dog distract, or Monky sick:
> That with more care keep holy-day
> The wrong, then others the right way:
> Compound for Sins, they are inclin'd to,
> By damning those they have no mind to;
> Still so perverse and opposite,
> As if they worshipp'd God for spight. (I. i. 187–216)

Unburdened by learning such as his master displays, the squire places his trust in inspiration.

> Whate're men speak by this *new Light*,
> Still they are sure to be i'th' right.
> 'Tis a *dark-Lanthorn* of the Spirit,
> Which none see by but those that bear it:
> A Light that falls down from on high,
> For Spiritual Trades to cousen by:
> An *Ignis Fatuus*, that bewitches,
> And leads men into Pools and Ditches.
>
> (I. i. 497–504)

In their different styles, both men are zealous and self-righteous Puritans.

This being so, they disapprove of such popular sports as bear-baiting, and their first adventure results from an attempt to suppress a match. In making the attempt, the knight and squire remind us of Don Quixote and Sancho Panza, and Butler undoubtedly owed something to Cervantes. He does not limit himself to the low burlesque in his description of the rough-and-tumble that ensues. When Hudibras tries to shoot Talgol the butcher,

> bending Cock, he level'd full
> Against th'outside of *Talgol*'s Skull;
> Vowing that he should ne're stir further,
> Nor henceforth Cow or Bullock murther.
> But *Pallas* came in shape of Rust,
> And 'twixt the Spring and Hammer thrust
> Her *Gorgon*-shield, which made the Cock
> Stand stiff as if 'twere turn'd t'a stock.
>
> (I. ii. 777–84)

The intervention by the goddess Pallas is mock-heroic, and mock-heroic features recur frequently throughout the poem. Butler can also indulge in mock-lyric, as when he permits Hudibras to express himself in the extravagant conceits favoured by contemporary love-poets (II. i. 553–82). But low burlesque predominates. In his account of the bear-baiting incident, Butler renders the conflict between Puritan censoriousness and turbulent humanity in terms of the simplest and crudest farce. The assault on Ralpho's horse by Magnano the tinker illustrates this:

> by foul hap having found
> Where Thistles grew on barren ground,
> In haste he drew his weapon out
> And having crop'd them from the Root
> He clapp'd them under th'Horses Tail
> With prickles sharper then a Nail.
> The angry Beast did straight resent
> The wrong done to his Fundament,
> Begun to kick, and fling, and wince,
> As if h' had been beside his sense,
> Striving to disengage from Smart,
> And raging Pain, th'afflicted Part.
> Instead of which he threw the pack
> Of *Squire* and baggage from his back.

(I. ii. 839–52)

Part I ends with Hudibras in the stocks. After his release, he courts a widow for her property, hoping for help from an astrologer and a lawyer; and incidentally he attempts to break up a popular folk ceremony – a Skimmington, such as Hardy was to introduce two centuries later into *The Mayor of Casterbridge* – just as he earlier tried to suppress a popular sport. He suffers cudgelling and humiliation.

All three parts contain also lengthy debates between his squire and himself, in which the Presbyterian's clumsy erudition contrasts with the Independent's enthusiastic reliance upon the inner light. Butler ludicrously echoes the cant of Puritanism, as when Ralpho directs his skill in casuistry to enabling Hudibras to break an oath. Placing a heavy emphasis upon the words 'in vain' in the commandment against swearing, he assures his master:

> W' are not commanded to forbear,
> Indefinitely, at all to *swear*,
> But to *swear* idly, and in vain,
> Without self-interest, or gain.
> For, breaking of an *Oath* and *Lying*,
> Is but a kind of *Self-denying*,
> A *Saint-like virtue*, and from hence,
> Some have broke *Oaths*, by *Providence*:
> Some, to the *Glory of the Lord*,
> *Perjur'd* themselves, and broke their word.
>
> (II. ii. 129–38)

Writing as a practical and reasonable man, Butler castigates the self-seeking, charlatanism and hypocrisy of the fanatics of his age. His style, for which he probably owed something to Scarron, is as unpretentious as it well could be. Except when the adoption of a particular jargon will serve a special purpose, his language is plain and idiomatic. His imagery is correspondingly homely and ordinary. His verse tumbles and bumps along with aggressive inelegance. His rhymes range from the facetiously ingenious, through the unremarkable, to the impudently makeshift, achieving at their most extravagant such combinations as *envy/men vye* (I. ii. 835–6), *subdue/tub to* (I. iii. 1023–4), *body/Custody* (II. i. 33–4), *famous else/Damosels* (II. i. 783–4), *Apostles/lost else* (II. ii. 775–6), and *inch is/Green Cheese* (II. iii. 265–6). Between this throw-away doggerel and the important subject Butler has chosen, the incongruity is extreme enough to make *Hudibras* a classical instance of the low burlesque.

During the eighteenth century and the early part of the nineteenth century, many imitators tried to emulate its success. But *Hudibras* itself flags in Part III, and Butler's followers did not come even as close as that to his original triumph. Less derivative poets, too, showed his influence when they used the octosyllabic couplet. Swift, for example, though writing in a smoother, less crotchety, less wayward manner than Butler's, leaves us in no doubt of his indebtedness to him in the passage quoted in Chapter 2 from 'Baucis and Philemon'. Its final rhyme, in particular, is genuinely Hudibrastic.

The use of this term to refer to a particular verse style, or even a particular kind of rhyme, will perhaps suggest that we need a different term to refer to the kind of low burlesque we are now discussing. But so many of the English low burlesques of any literary merit belong to the period inaugurated by *Hudibras*, and are written in the metrical form and literary style of *Hudibras*, that the attempt to substitute a new term would inevitably be somewhat arbitrary. At the same time, we must recognize that there are works which pursue broadly the same tactics as *Hudibras* without employing its metrical form and literary style. Such tactics are sometimes adopted today in the satirical sketches included in variety shows. But for a long time the Hudibrastic type of burlesque has ceased to have even such literary pretensions as it had in its heyday.

4
Parody

A high-minded critic has spoken of 'the vulgar craft of parody'. Perhaps the popularity of this kind of burlesque prompted his choice of epithet. At all events, the popularity is considerable, and it has developed relatively recently. While parodies have survived from earlier periods, the modern vogue effectively begins in this country with John Philips' 'The Splendid Shilling' (1701), a short parody of *Paradise Lost*. Philips uses Miltonic blank verse to bewail his own lack of splendid shillings:

> Thus do I live from Pleasure quite debarr'd,
> Nor taste the Fruits that the Sun's genial Rays
> Mature, *John-Apple*, nor the downy *Peach*,
> Nor *Walnut* in rough-furrow'd Coat secure,
> Nor *Medlar*, Fruit delicious in Decay.

His very breeches are worn through:

> My *Galligaskins* that have long withstood
> The Winter's Fury, and Encroaching Frosts,
> By Time subdu'd, (what will not Time subdue!)
> An horrid Chasm disclose, with Orifice
> Wide, Discontinuous; at which the Winds
> *Eurus* and *Auster*, and the dreadful Force
> Of *Boreas*, that congeals the *Cronian* Waves,
> Tumultuous enter with dire chilling Blasts,
> Portending Agues.

By placing Milton's grand manner at the disposal of humble and private concerns, Philips creates the incongruity in which burlesque consists.

Thirty-five years later, another pioneering work appeared. This was Isaac Hawkins Browne's *A Pipe of Tobacco* (1736), our earliest collection of parodies of various authors, all supposed to be writing on a single subject. Browne imitates Edward Young, Swift and Pope with particular fidelity. Pope admired his skill and found no offence in its application to himself:

> Blest Leaf! whose aromatic Gales dispense
> To Templars Modesty, to Parsons Sense:
> So raptur'd Priests, at fam'd *Dodona*'s Shrine
> Drank Inspiration from the Steam divine.
> Poison that cures, a Vapour that affords
> Content, more solid than the Smile of Lords:
> Rest to the Weary, to the Hungry Food,
> The last kind Refuge of the WISE and GOOD: ...
> Come to thy Poet, come with healing Wings,
> And let me taste Thee unexcis'd by Kings.

Browne's parodies lack bite; they are the innocuous products of literary play. A wish to serve a serious purpose, coupled with a touch of malice towards the victim, gives much greater incisiveness to George Canning's parodies of Southey. These first appeared in *The Anti-Jacobin* (1797–8), a periodical founded by Canning to combat the subversive principles in philosophy and politics that were current at the time and that the French revolutionaries had been putting into effect. At this date Southey, later to be castigated by Byron as a reactionary, still believed in these principles. He naturally attracted the attention of the brilliant young Tory who was in due course to become Foreign Secretary and Prime Minister.

Southey had published a sentimental humanitarian poem in sapphics, 'The Widow', which starts

> Cold was the night wind, drifting fast the snows fell,
> Wide were the downs and shelterless and naked,
> When a poor Wanderer struggled on her journey
>   Weary and way-sore.

Her appeals for help evoke no response from travellers passing in a coach and on horseback, and the widow dies from exposure. Canning, in 'The Friend of Humanity and the Knife-Grinder', also in sapphics, entrusts the humanitarian sentiments to an egalitarian and republican Friend of Humanity:

> Needy Knife-grinder! whither are you going?
> Rough is the road, your Wheel is out of order –
> Bleak blows the blast; – your hat has got a hole in't,
>   So have your breeches!
>
> Weary Knife-grinder! little think the proud ones,
> Who in their coaches roll along the turnpike-
> road, what hard work 'tis crying all day 'Knives and
>   Scissars to grind O!'
>
> Tell me, Knife-grinder, how you came to grind knives?
> Did some rich man tyrannically use you?
> Was it the 'Squire? or Parson of the Parish?
>   Or the Attorney? . . .
>
> (Have you not read the Rights of Man, by TOM PAINE?)
> Drops of compassion tremble on my eye-lids,
> Ready to fall, as soon as you have told your
>   Pitiful story.

But the Knife-grinder does not respond to this direct invitation to feed his questioner's sentimentalism:

> Story! God bless you! I have none to tell, Sir,
> Only last night a-drinking at the Chequers,
> This poor old hat and breeches, as you see, were
>   Torn in a scuffle.

Declaring, 'I never love to meddle/With Politics, Sir', he tries to cadge sixpence. The Friend of Humanity swells with indignation:

> *I* give thee Sixpence! I will see thee damn'd first –
> Wretch! whom no sense of wrongs can rouse to vengeance –

> Sordid, unfeeling, reprobate, degraded,
>   Spiritless outcast!
>
> (*Kicks the Knife-grinder, overturns his Wheel, and exit in a transport of republican enthusiasm and universal philanthropy.*)

Canning's scorn for the cant of revolutionism found renewed expression later in the same year, 1797, in 'The Soldier's Friend', a parody of Southey's poem in dactylics, 'The Soldier's Wife'.

The most famous successor to Hawkins Browne's collection of parodic variations on a theme came in 1812. Drury Lane Theatre had been burned down three years earlier, and the committee in charge advertised for an address to be recited at the opening of the present building. The committee liked none of the 112 addresses submitted to it and commissioned Byron to write one. The brothers Horace and James Smith saw an opportunity for parody and published *Rejected Addresses*, a collection of twenty-one items allegedly by various eminent hands.

These display a remarkable variety. Three of them are travesties, the most entertaining being that of Macbeth's soliloquy, 'Is this a dagger which I see before me' (II. i). But parodies make up the bulk of the volume and give it its main interest. The Smiths' Wordsworth is a lyrical balladist, flatfootedly versifying the obvious:

> Well, after many a sad reproach,
> They got into a hackney coach,
>   And trotted down the street.
> I saw them go: one horse was blind,
> The tails of both hung down behind,
>   Their shoes were on their feet;

their Byron is a theatrically pessimistic Childe Harold:

> Ye reckless dupes, who hither wend your way
> To gaze on puppets in a painted dome,
> Pursuing pastimes glittering to betray,
> Like falling stars in life's eternal gloom,
> What seek ye here? Joy's evanescent bloom?

their Cobbett, combative and prejudiced, introduces his address by declaring, 'To the gewgaw fetters of *rhyme* (invented by the monks to enslave the people) I have a rooted objection. I have therefore written an address for your Theatre in plain, homespun, yeoman's *prose*'; their Moore shifts, in the lilting rhythm associated with his name, from celebrating 'woman's soft smile' to lauding the natives of 'the Emerald Isle of the ocean'; their Scott is brisk, clangorous, and appropriately antiquarian; and their Coleridge ruminates in flaccid blank verse. Perhaps their Crabbe is their finest achievement. A dogged realist, Crabbe himself had seemed to Byron, 'Though Nature's sternest Painter, yet the best' (*English Bards, and Scotch Reviewers*, l. 858); in view of his habitual employment of the eighteenth-century heroic couplet, James Smith described him, in a footnote to the parody, as 'Pope in worsted stockings'. The parody incorporates a tale in verse, which opens in Crabbe's most deliberately truthful manner:

> John Richard William Alexander Dwyer
> Was footman to Justinian Stubbs, Esquire;
> But when John Dwyer listed in the Blues,
> Emanuel Jennings polish'd Stubbs's shoes.
> Emanuel Jennings brought his youngest boy
> Up as a corn-cutter – a safe employ;
> In Holywell Street, St. Pancras, he was bred
> (At number twenty-seven, it is said),
> Facing the pump, and near the Granby's Head:
> He would have bound him to some shop in town,
> But with a premium he could not come down.
> Pat was the urchin's name – a red-hair'd youth,
> Fonder of purl and skittle-grounds than truth.

Of all these scrupulously recorded names, only the last, Pat Jennings, is relevant to the narrative they introduce.

The Smiths' victims took their pillorying in good part. Byron told Lady Blessington that whereas parodies normally give a bad impression of their originals the opposite is the case with *Rejected*

Addresses, 'and he quoted the second and third stanzas, in imitation of himself, as admirable, and just what he could have wished to write on a similar subject' (*Lady Blessington's 'Conversations of Lord Byron'*, ed. E. J. Lovell, Princeton, 1969, pp. 83–4). Scott, as recorded in Horace Smith's preface to the eighteenth edition (1833), went even further. He pointed to the description of the fire in the parody of himself and said, 'I certainly must have written this myself – although I forget upon what occasion.'

With *The Anti-Jacobin* and *Rejected Addresses*, parody in English attained maturity. Since then it has flourished on both sides of the Atlantic, though the development came more slowly in the United States than in Great Britain. Most of the principal writers have received the teasing, if also flattering, attentions of parodists. Some of them have made their own contributions to the form. In a letter dated 23 August 1821, Byron protested against the parsimony of his publisher, John Murray, in verses echoing Cowper's 'To Mary'; and Swinburne not only ridiculed Tennyson's 'The Higher Pantheism' in 'The Higher Pantheism in a Nutshell' but in 'Nephelidia' deliberately parodied himself.

'Nephelidia' ingeniously exaggerates the hypnotic rhythm and the mechanical alliteration characteristic of Swinburne's writing. A really critical parody would strike more deeply, however, and A. C. Hilton's burlesque of Swinburne's 'Dolores' does just this. 'Dolores', a fevered expression of the nineteenth-century cult of the Fatal Woman, had an extraordinary reputation among young Victorians. Like many of Swinburne's poems, it is too long. Two of its fifty-five stanzas will suffice for present purposes:

> Cold eyelids that hide like a jewel
>   Hard eyes that grow soft for an hour;
> The heavy white limbs, and the cruel
>   Red mouth like a venomous flower;
> When these are gone by with their glories,
>   What shall rest of thee then, what remain,

O mystic and sombre Dolores,
  Our Lady of Pain? ...

O lips full of lust and of laughter,
  Curled snakes that are fed from my breast,
Bite hard, lest remembrance come after
  And press with new lips where you pressed.
For my heart too springs up at the pressure,
  Mine eyelids too moisten and burn;
Ah, feed me and fill me with pleasure,
  Ere pain come in turn.

Hilton does not merely borrow Swinburne's metrical form and verse style; he follows him in addressing masochistic sentiments to a predator. But not even Swinburne could long to surrender to such a predator as his. The incongruity between his subject and his style provokes laughter, and this helps us to perceive in a clearer critical light both Swinburne's style and the feelings with which he regards his subject. Here are the first and last of Hilton's five stanzas entitled 'Octopus':

Strange beauty, eight-limbed and eight-handed,
  Whence camest to dazzle our eyes?
With thy bosom bespangled and banded
  With the hues of the seas and the skies;
Is thy home European or Asian,
  O mystical monster marine?
Part molluscous and partly crustacean,
  Betwixt and between. ...

Ah! thy red lips, lascivious and luscious,
  With death in their amorous kiss,
Cling round us, and clasp us, and crush us,
  With bitings of agonised bliss;
We are sick with the poison of pleasure,
  Dispense us the potion of pain;
Ope thy mouth to its uttermost measure
  And bite us again!

In much the same way, Hugh Kingsmill not only reflects Housman's lyrical manner but also carries to a ludicrous extreme his defiant pessimism and Stoical acquiescence in death:

> What, still alive at twenty-two
> A clean upstanding chap like you?
> Sure, if your throat 'tis hard to slit,
> Slit your girl's, and swing for it;

Lewis Carroll employs the metrical form and verse style of Tennyson's 'The Two Voices' to project anxious doubts and ponderings similar to Tennyson's upon an incongruously prosaic subject-matter:

> 'To dine!' she sneered in acid tone,
> 'To bend thy being to a bone
> Clothed in a radiance not its own!'
>
> The tear-drop trickled to his chin:
> There was a meaning in her grin
> That made him feel on fire within.
>
> 'Term it not "radiance",' said he:
> ''Tis solid nutriment to me.
> Dinner is Dinner: Tea is Tea.'
>
> And she, 'Yea so? Yet wherefore cease!
> Let thy scant knowledge find increase.
> Say "Men are Men, and Geese are Geese".'
>
> He moaned: he knew not what to say.
> The thought 'That I could get away!'
> Strove with the thought 'But I must stay' . . .
>
> Pitying his obvious distress,
> Yet with a tinge of bitterness,
> She said 'The More exceeds the Less'.
>
> 'A truth of such undoubted weight',
> He urged, 'and so extreme in date,
> It were superfluous to state.'

Roused into sudden passion, she
In tone of cold malignity:
'To others, yea: but not to thee.'

('The Three Voices')

and Henry Reed reproduces both the literary mannerisms and the modes of thought and feeling characteristic of T. S. Eliot in *Four Quartets*:

As we get older we do not get any younger.
Seasons return, and today I am fifty-five,
And this time last year I was fifty-four,
And this time next year I shall be sixty-two.
And I cannot say I should like (to speak for myself)
To see my time over again – if you can call it time:
Fidgeting uneasily under a draughty stair,
Or counting sleepless nights in the crowded tube.

Eliot himself acknowledged the accuracy and point of 'Chard Whitlow', from which these lines come.

As we have already seen, however, many parodies are not designed to make any serious critical point. A lively modern instance is Ezra Pound's exuberant burlesque of the thirteenth-century lyric, 'Sumer is icumen in:/Lhude sing, cuccu!' It expresses an American's impatience with the British weather:

Winter is icummen in,
Lhude sing Goddamm,
Raineth drop and staineth slop,
And how the wind doth ramm!
        Sing: Goddamm.
Skiddeth bus and sloppeth us,
An ague hath my ham.
Freezeth river, turneth liver,
        Damn you, sing: Goddamm.
Goddamm, Goddamm, 'tis why I am, Goddamm,
        So 'gainst the winter's balm.
Sing goddamm, damm, sing Goddamm,
Sing goddamm, sing goddamm, DAMM.

With the exception of the Smiths' address in the style of Cobbett, all the parodies considered so far have been verse parodies. But prose parodies, too, have a long history. Shakespeare enables Falstaff to mimic Lyly's *Euphues* in *I Henry IV* (1597), II. iv. Swift's *Meditation upon a Broom-Stick* (1708) echoes and ridicules 'the heavenly meditations' of Robert Boyle. As chaplain to the Earl of Berkeley, Swift tired of reading these aloud to his employer's wife and successfully passed off his own piece to her as genuine. When the truth came out, she laughed good-naturedly: 'What a vile trick that rogue played me. But it is his way, he never balks his humour in any thing.'

In the anonymous *Shamela* (1741), apparently by Henry Fielding, we have a complete parodic novel. Richardson's *Pamela, or Virtue Rewarded*, published late in the previous year, tells how a young maidservant, whose mistress has just died, repels the dishonourable and even violent advances of the lady's son, until the young man capitulates and proposes marriage. Richardson evidently saw this proposal as the reward for Pamela's long-suffering virtue; others saw it as marking Pamela's success in extorting the full price for the commodity she has to offer.

Fielding saw it this way and supplied in *Shamela* his own sardonically realistic account of the affair. Naturally, he follows Richardson in writing an epistolary novel. Shamela's second letter expresses her readiness to respond to her master's attentions:

Dear Mamma,
O what News, since I writ my last! the young Squire hath been here, and as sure as a Gun he hath taken a Fancy to me; *Pamela*, says he, (for so I am called here) you was a great Favourite of your late Mistress's; yes, an't please your Honour, says I; and I believe you deserved it, says he; thank your Honour for your good Opinion, says I; and then he took me by the Hand, and I pretended to be shy: Laud, says I, Sir, I hope you don't intend to be rude; no, says he, my Dear, and then he kissed me, 'till he took away my Breath – and I pretended to be Angry, and to get away, and then he kissed me again, and

breathed very short, and looked very silly; and by Ill-Luck Mrs. *Jervis* came in, and had like to have spoiled Sport. – *How troublesome is such Interruption!* You shall hear now soon, for I shall not come away yet, so I rest,

Your affectionate Daughter,

SHAMELA.

Before long, Shamela realizes that her natural assets will fetch a high price if she disposes of them prudently. In Letter X she asks,

Now, Mamma, what think you? – For my own Part, I am convinced he will marry me, and faith so he shall. O! Bless me! I shall be Mrs. *Booby*, and be Mistress of a great Estate, and have a dozen Coaches and Six, and a fine House at *London*, and another at *Bath*, and Servants, and Jewels, and Plate, and go to Plays, and Opera's, and Court; and do what I will, and spend what I will.

To whet her master's appetite, she prates a good deal about her virtue, giving the word the fashionable pronunciation indicated by its spelling:

Pamela, says he, . . . you see I cannot stay long from you, which I think is a sufficient Proof of the Violence of my Passion. Yes, Sir, says I, I see your Honour intends to ruin me, that nothing but the Destruction of my Vartue will content you.

O what a charming Word that is, rest his Soul who first invented it.

How can you say I would ruin you, answered the Squire, when you shall not ask any thing which I will not grant you. If that be true, says I, good your Honour let me go Home to my poor but honest Parents; that is all I have to ask, and do not ruin a poor Maiden, who is resolved to carry her Vartue to the Grave with her.

Hussy, says he, don't provoke me, don't provoke me, I say. You are absolutely in my power, and if you won't let me lie with you by fair Means, I will by Force. O la, Sir, says I, I don't understand your paw [i.e., improper] Words. – Very pretty Treatment indeed, says he, to say I use paw Words; Hussy, Gipsie, Hypocrite, Saucebox, Boldface, get out of my Sight, or I will lend you such a Kick in the – I don't care to repeat the Word, but he meant my hinder part.

(Letter X)

At the end of the same letter, Shamela can reflect, 'I thought once of making a little Fortune by my Person. I now intend to make a great one by my Vartue.' For a time at least, she succeeds in this aim.

Early in 1742, within a year of the appearance of *Shamela*, Fielding published *Joseph Andrews*. This, too, is a parody of *Pamela*, though much less exclusively so than its predecessor. In it, Fielding reverses the sex of the two main characters: Lady Booby is the pursuer, and her intended quarry is Pamela's innocent brother, whose name recalls the Joseph who fled from Potiphar's wife in Genesis xxxix. No doubt Fielding's contemporaries found it particularly absurd to have a vigorous young man harp on his virtue as Joseph does in a letter to his sister:

> *Dear Sister* Pamela,
>
> Hoping you are well, what News have I to tell you! O *Pamela*, my Mistress is fallen in love with me – That is, what great Folks call falling in love, she has a mind to ruin me; but I hope, I shall have more Resolution and more Grace than to part with my Virtue to any Lady upon Earth. . . .
>
> I don't doubt, dear Sister, but you will have Grace to preserve your Virtue against all Trials; and I beg you earnestly to pray, I may be enabled to preserve mine: for truly, it is very severely attacked by more than one: but, I hope I shall copy your Example, and that of *Joseph*, my Name's-sake; and maintain my Virtue against all Temptations.
>
> (I. x)

Despite Fielding's inclusion of a couple of letters to Pamela from her brother, *Joseph Andrews* is not an epistolary novel. Nor is it consistently a parody: other interests dominate its central chapters, and there are naturally many mock-heroic passages in 'a comic Epic-Poem in Prose' ('Preface'). When all has been said, however, there is no denying the closeness of its relationship to Richardson's book.

The finest prose parodist in English is probably Max Beerbohm. In 'The Guerdon' he writes from the point of view of a Lord Chamberlain who is in attendance while his monarch looks over an honours list that includes a name which neither of them recognizes but which neither of them will admit to not recognizing. The name is that of the author whose style is being parodied: Henry James. As the Lord Chamberlain approaches the palace, he faces the fact of his ignorance:

> He hadn't the beginning of a notion – since it had been a point of pride with him, as well as of urbanity, not to ask – who the fellow, the so presumably illustrious and deserving chap in question *was*. This omission so loomed for him that he was to be conscious, as he came to the end of the great moist avenue, of a felt doubt as to whether he could, in his bemusement, now 'place' anybody at all; to which condition of his may have been due the impulse that, at the reached gates of the palace, caused him to pause and all vaguely, all peeringly inquire of one of the sentries: 'To whom do you beautifully belong?'

With its elaborations and hesitations and qualifications, this contrasts sharply with the bluntly provincial 'Scruts', in which Arnold Bennett is Beerbohm's victim:

> Since Jos Wrackgarth had introduced him to his sister at the Hanbridge Oddfellows' Biennial Hop, when he danced two quadrilles with her, he had seen her but once. He had nodded to her, Five Towns fashion, and she had nodded back at him, but with a look that seemed to say 'You needn't nod next time you see me. I can get along well enough without your nods.' A frightening girl! And yet her brother had since told him she seemed 'a bit gone, like' on him. Impossible! He, Albert Grapp, make an impression on the brilliant Miss Wrackgarth! Yet she had sent him a verbal invite to spend Christmas in her own home. And the time had come. He was on his way. Incredible that he should arrive! The tram must surely overturn, or be struck by lightning. And yet no! He arrived safely.
>
> The small servant who opened the door gave him another verbal message from Miss Wrackgarth. It was that he must wipe his feet 'well' on the mat. In obeying this order he experienced a thrill of satisfaction

he could not account for. He must have stood shuffling his boots vigorously for a full minute. This, he told himself, was life. He, Albert Grapp, was alive. And the world was full of other men, all alive; and yet, because they were not doing Miss Wrackgarth's bidding, none of them really lived. He was filled with a vague melancholy. But his melancholy pleased him.

In the parlour he found Jos awaiting him. The table was laid for three.

'So you're here, are you?' said the host, using the Five Towns formula. 'Emily's in the kitchen,' he added. 'Happen she'll be here directly.'

'I hope she's tol-lol-ish?' asked Albert.

'She is,' said Jos. 'But don't you go saying that to her. She doesn't care about society airs and graces. You'll make no headway if you aren't blunt.'

Perhaps the most widely enjoyed of all twentieth-century burlesques of novels is Stella Gibbons' *Cold Comfort Farm* (1932). This describes country life in Sussex in the kind of language favoured by Mary Webb and other modern primitivists. Between Adam Lambsbreath and the farm animals, for example, there was 'a close bond: a slow, deep, primitive, silent down-dragging link between Adam and all living beasts; they knew each other's simple needs. They lay close to the earth, and something of earth's old fierce simplicities had seeped into their beings.' A page or two later, we learn that Seth Starkadder's voice 'had a low, throaty, animal quality, a sneering warmth that wound a velvet ribbon of sexuality over the outward coarseness of the man.' Meriam, the hired girl, is pregnant by Seth. 'Was it not February, and the earth a-teem with newing life?' (iii). Such passages catch perfectly the blood-and-soil sentimentalism that Stella Gibbons mocks.

Is her novel accurately labelled a parody? In so far as she is ridiculing a particular author, it is. But Mary Webb is not the only primitivist whom we recall as we read. Thomas Hardy, J. C. Powys, and D. H. Lawrence also come to our minds. In so far as

Stella Gibbons is burlesquing a whole *genre*, *Cold Comfort Farm* may claim to be a variant, in a period dominated by its prose literature, of the mock-poem that had flourished two hundred years earlier.

In the 'Oxen of the Sun' episode of *Ulysses*, Joyce shows himself an extraordinarily versatile imitator of prose styles. The episode describes Leopold Bloom's visit to a maternity hospital to ask after Mrs Purefoy. He there meets a convivial group of young men, including Stephen Dedalus, and accompanies them when they leave for a night out together.

Since the setting is a maternity hospital, the theme of growth or development naturally prevails. To provide a suitable prose medium for it, Joyce chooses to imitate in roughly chronological order a wide variety of English styles from the primitive to the contemporary. Many readers have found this choice of technique too deliberate, the artifice of it too patent; but there is no denying the skill of the *pastiches*. That of Sir Thomas Browne finally breaks down into absurdity, but until this happens it reproduces perfectly the rich diction, the incantatory rhythm, and the grave tone of its original:

> And as the ends and ultimates of all things accord in some mean and measure with their inceptions and originals, that same multiplicit concordance which leads forth growth from birth accomplishing by a retrogressive metamorphosis that minishing and ablation towards the final which is agreeable unto nature, so is it with our subsolar being. The aged sisters draw us into life: we wail, batten, sport, clip, clasp, sunder, dwindle, die: over us dead they bend. First saved from water of old Nile, among bulrushes, a bed of fasciated wattles: at last the cavity of a mountain, an occulted sepulchre amid the conclamation of the hillcat and the ossifrage. And as no man knows the ubicity of his tumulus nor to what processes we shall thereby be ushered nor whether to Tophet or to Edenville in the like way is all hidden when we would backward see from what region of remoteness the whatness of our whoness hath fetched his whenceness.

A little later, in the style of Pepys, Joyce repeats the names of the men who come together at the hospital: 'There Leop. Bloom of Crawford's journal sitting snug with a covey of wags, likely brangling fellows, Dixon jun., scholar of my lady of Mercy, Vin. Lynch, a Scots fellow, Will. Madden, T. Lenehan, very sad for a racinghorse he fancied, and Stephen D.' But Pepys is a readily imitable writer. Joyce achieves something more rare when he mimics Dickens. He represents the novelist not in his comic but in his lingeringly and repetitiously sentimental vein:

> Meanwhile the skill and patience of the physician had brought about a happy *accouchement*. It had been a weary weary while both for patient and doctor. All that surgical skill could do was done and the brave woman had manfully helped. She had. She had fought the good fight and now she was very very happy. Those who have passed on, who have gone before, are happy too as they gaze down and smile upon the touching scene. Reverently look at her as she reclines there with the motherlight in her eyes, that longing hunger for baby fingers (a pretty sight it is to see), in the first bloom of her new motherhood, breathing a silent prayer of thanksgiving to One above, the Universal Husband. And as her loving eyes behold her babe she wishes only one blessing more, to have her dear Doady there with her to share her joy, to lay in his arms that mite of God's clay, the fruit of their lawful embraces.

Such details as the incongruous 'manfully' and the extravagant 'Universal Husband' here tip imitation decisively into parody. In the passage after Browne, however, only the final phrase has this effect; otherwise, the thought and feeling and the language are alike such as Browne might himself have acknowledged. Much of the 'Oxen of the Sun' episode relates in this direct fashion to its literary models. On the whole, Joyce is not essaying burlesque; he is not lavishing his English literary styles upon subjects with which he believes them ludicrously incongruous. Though he sedulously imitates his models, he parodies them only intermittently.

Admittedly, parody is already obvious when he describes a tin of sardines in the voice of the fourteenth-century compiler of travellers' tales known as Sir John Mandeville:

> And there was a vat of silver that was moved by craft to open in the which lay strange fishes withouten heads though misbelieving men nie that this be possible thing without they see it natheless they are so. And these fishes lie in an oily water brought there from Portugal land because of the fatness that therein is like to the juices of the olive press.

Joyce clearly enjoys wedding the marvelling tone with the commonplace sense of this. But he has also serious business on hand. In the *Odyssey*, father and son are reunited only in the hut of Eumaeus after the father's return to Ithaca. In *Ulysses*, Leopold Bloom and Stephen Dedalus come together at the hospital. 'And sir Leopold sat with them', writes Joyce in the gravely courteous manner of Sir Thomas Malory, 'for he bore fast friendship to sir Simon and to this his son young Stephen and for that his languor becalmed him there after longest wanderings insomuch as they feasted him for that time in the honourablest manner.' This theme accompanies the theme of growth or development from these opening pages to the end of the episode, and its prominence increases in the 'Circe', 'Eumaeus', and 'Ithaca' episodes which follow. When the 'likely brangling fellows' rush from the hospital to Burke's pub, Joyce resorts to the exclamatory impressionism of Carlyle, especially as exemplified in *The French Revolution*; and he concludes the episode with an incoherent gabble of contemporary speech as they lapse into drunkenness.

In this part of *Ulysses*, then, we have a sequence of imitations which can become parodic, and hilariously so, but serve primarily to carry forward serious themes. For imitations which are as nearly free from parody as seems possible, we may turn to *An Italian Visit* (1953), by Cecil Day Lewis. In Part V of this, Day Lewis writes poems on five works of art he saw in Florence, employing for each of them the congenial style of a recent and admired poet. Donatello's *Judith and Holofernes*, he feels, calls for the manner of W. B. Yeats in such poems as 'The Tower':

> Next, a rich widow woman comes to mind
> Who, when her folk were starving, dined and wined
> Alone with Holofernes, until he
> Grew rabid for her flesh. And presently,
> Matching deceit with bitterer deceit,
> She had struck off that tipsy captain's head
> Upon the still untousled bed,
> And borne it homeward in a bag of meat.

The haughty rhetoric of this contrasts with the poet's coolly humorous distancing of himself from the action when reviewing Piero di Cosimo's *Perseus Rescuing Andromeda* in the manner of W. H. Auden:

> It is all there. The victim broods,
> Her friends take up the attitudes
>   Right for disaster;
> The winsome rescuer draws his sword,
> While from the svelte, impassive fjord
> Breaches terrific, dense and bored
>   The usual monster.

Imitations as faithful as these inevitably prompt criticisms of the authors imitated. But Day Lewis is not in any way creating that incongruity between subject and style which makes for burlesque. His five poems are almost the poems that his five poets might themselves have written.

As when discussing travesty, I have considered borderline instances, and even instances which fall just outside the range of my immediate topic, with the purpose of defining precisely how much that topic covers. Following a brief sketch of the development of English parody between 1701 and 1812, I have relinquished the historical approach and have tried simply to illustrate and discuss something of the variety of the parodies written during the nineteenth and twentieth centuries. I have reviewed parodies in verse and parodies in prose; playful parodies and critical parodies; and parodies in which the requisite incongruity springs strictly from the choice of unworthy subjects, as distinct from parodies, such as Joyce's rendering of Dickens, in which it springs mainly from the deliberate heightening of the victim's style.

Inevitably, many accomplished practitioners have escaped mention. Before the twentieth century, James Hogg, William Aytoun, Bayard Taylor, C. S. Calverley, Thomas Hood the younger, H. D. Traill, and J. K. Stephen all did work from which I might well have drawn. In the early years of the present century, Owen Seaman and J. C. Squire were deservedly popular. Some of the finest modern parodies have come from members of the American *New Yorker* school. Of these, Robert Benchley, Peter DeVries, Wolcott Gibbs, S. J. Perelman, Frank Sullivan, James Thurber, and E. B. White receive honourable mention in the useful essay Dwight Macdonald appends to his *Parodies: An Anthology from Chaucer to Beerbohm – and After* (1961). Most of them are represented in his collection.

5
The Mock-Poem

High burlesque flourished in the Classical literature of Greece and Rome. The plays of Aristophanes contain parodies of Euripides and others, and one of the most famous of all mock-poems is the *Batrachomyomachia*, or *Battle of the Frogs and the Mice*. This Greek mock-epic of unknown but certainly post-Homeric date long passed under Homer's name. It ascribes the hostilities which form its subject to the destruction of a mouse while the guest of a frog, and it shows how the Olympian deities interest themselves in the strife.

Mock-heroism recurs in medieval literature. When the hen Pertelote rebukes the pusillanimous cock Chauntecleer in Chaucer's *Nun's Priest's Tale* by asking the rhetorical question, 'Have ye no mannes herte, and han a berd?', the incongruity which runs through the whole poem is momentarily focused in a single line. But *The Nun's Priest's Tale* does not have the full epic machinery and style.

Nor can we say that *La Secchia Rapita* (*The Rape of the Bucket*, 1622) maintains a consistently mock-epic tone, though Alessandro Tassoni, its author, claimed to have originated the modern mock-epic, and though his claim was allowed by a consensus of his successors' opinions. The poem deals with the seizure of a wooden bucket from a Bolognese well by the vanguard of a Modenese army during a war between the two cities. Like the Helen of the *Iliad*, the bucket is the prize for which the combatants struggle. Tassoni promises,

> vedrai, s'al cantar mio porgi l'orecchia,
> Elene trasformarsi in una secchia. (I. ii)

> (You'll see, if you're attentive to my tale,
> Helen of Troy transformed into a pail.)

As in the *Iliad* and the *Batrachomyomachia*, the gods take sides; Venus, Bacchus and Mars support the Modenese, Pallas and Phoebus the Bolognese. Whereas Tassoni normally employs high burlesque in presenting his human characters and their bucket, he resorts to low burlesque in presenting the gods.

A half-century later, Boileau produced a mock-poem that followed more strictly the example of the epic. Towards the end of his *Discourse concerning the Original and Progress of Satire* (1693), Dryden writes well on Boileau's relationship to Tassoni:

> The *Secchia Rapita*, is an Italian Poem; a Satire of the *Varronian* kind. 'Tis written in the Stanza of Eight, which is their Measure for Heroique Verse. The Words are stately, the Numbers smooth, the Turn both of Thoughts and Words is happy. The first six lines of the Stanza seem Majestical and Severe: but the two last turn them all, into a pleasant Ridicule. *Boileau*, if I am not much deceiv'd, has model'd from hence, his famous *Lutrin*. He had read the Burlesque Poetry of *Scarron*, with some kind of Indignation, as witty as it was, and found nothing in *France* that was worthy of his Imitation. But he Copy'd the *Italian* so well, that his own may pass for an Original. He writes it in the *French* Heroique Verse, and calls it an Heroique Poem: His Subject is Trivial, but his Verse is Noble.

The trivial subject of *Le Lutrin* (from 1674) is the strife between a Prelate and a Chanter about the setting-up in the choir of the lectern which gives the poem its title. Boileau supplies the full epic treatment. He begins with a formal statement of his theme and then proceeds to invoke the muse:

> Muse, redy-moy donc quelle ardeur de vengeance,
> De ces Hommes sacrez rompit l'intelligence,
> Et troubla si long-temps deux celebres Rivaux.
> Tant de fiel entre-t-il dans l'ame des devots?

> (i. 9–12)

(Instruct me *Muse*, for thou canst tell, what Thirst
Of sweet Revenge, thô Dire, engaged first
Religious Souls to break the Sacred Tye
Of blessed Peace and heaven-born Amitie,
To make old Friends new Rivals; *can there rest*
Such bitter Gall in a Religious Breast?)

(tr. N.O., 1682)

In telling his story, he burlesques such characteristics of the classical epic as the set speeches, the expansive similes, the battles, and the supernatural agents.

In *Le Lutrin* these agents are allegorical figures. One of them, Night, leads an owl to hide herself in the lectern, which has been stored in the vestry for thirty years. The Prelate's men arrive under cover of darkness to instal it in the choir. One of them starts to move it.

Mais à peine il y touche, ô prodige incroyable!
Que du Pupitre sort une voix effroyable.
Brontin en est émû, le Sacristain paslit,
Le Perruquier commence à regretter son lit.
Dans son hardi projet toutefois il s'obstine:
Lorsque des flancs poudreux de la vaste machine
L'Oyseau sort en courroux, et d'un cri menaçant
Acheve d'étonner le Barbier fremissant.
De ses aîles dans l'air secoüant la poussiere,
Dans la main de Boirude il éteint la lumiere;
Les Guerriers à ce coup demeurent confondus:
Ils regagnent la Nef de frayeur éperdus.
Sous leurs corps tremblotans leurs genoux s'affoiblissent,
D'une subite horreur leurs cheveux se herissent,
Et bien-tost, au travers des ombres de la nuit,
Le timide Escadron se dissipe et s'enfuit.
    Ainsi lorsqu'en un coin, qui leur tient lieu d'azile,
D'Ecoliers libertins une troupe indocile,
Loin des yeux d'un Préfèt au travail assidu,
Va tenir quelquefois un Brelan deffendu:

D

Si du veillant Argus la figure effrayante
Dans l'ardeur du plaisir à leurs yeux se présente,
Le jeu cesse à l'instant, l'azile est deserté,
Et tout fuit à grands pas le Tyran redouté.

    La Discorde qui voit leur honteuse disgrace,
Dans les airs cependant tonne, éclate, menace,
Et malgré la frayeur dont leurs cœurs sont glacez,
S'appreste à réünir ses Soldats dispersez.

                         (iii. 69–96)

(He scarce had mov'd it, O portentous wonder!
When from its hollow womb a Voice did Thunder;
Brontin starts back! The Sexton lookt like Dead!
John with his Dear, twice wisht himself in Bed!
But on their purpose obstinately bent,
They roll it or'e, true Zeal will ne're relent!
Out flies the broad-fac'd Chorister of the Night,
And with her ruffling wings strikes out the Light:
This struck their Souls with horrible Confusion,
Amaz'd they stand, they doubt; but in conclusion,
As soon as Fear lent them the use of Feet
Away they trudge, fill'd with shame and Regret;
The Nave they soon recover; whil'st their hair
Stands bristling on their heads, dissolving fear
Makes their Knees quiver underneath their Bodies,
And there they sneaking stand like baffled Noddies,
Sheltred by the same Darkness brought them thither,
The Squadron flies at last, they knew not whither.
  So when a Jolly Crew of Truants gather
Into some Nook, to play their pranks together,
Secure of Eyes from Monitor and Master,
They burn the day in game, and sport the faster;
If now by chance, the Tyrants Eye doth watch 'em,
And unawares at Cards or Dice he catch 'em;
The sad surprize, their Mirth and Pastime dashes,
And each shifts for himself to scape his lashes.
Such was our Warriours plight when once the Owl
Sprung from the Pew, set up her Doleful howl.

Discord, who saw unseen their fowl disgrace,
Clapping her wings, pity'd their woful case:
Their Spirits quail'd, their Courages abated;
Rallies in hast the Troop disanimated.)

(tr. N.O., 1682)

Boileau ironically sustains a grave epic decorum in recounting
this ignominious flight by his 'Guerriers' ('warriors'). An epic
simile illustrates their panic, and Discord herself arrives to renew
their purpose. In his relaxed and rowdy English version, N.O.
sacrifices Boileau's briskness and restraint. His tone is humorous
and at times, as in the reference to 'baffled Noddies', decidedly
Hudibrastic. But Boileau disparaged the low burlesque and by his
example in *Le Lutrin* established the high burlesque in the esteem
of his English successors, Dryden, Garth and Pope. He, rather
than Tassoni, stimulated the development of the mock-epic in
England.

Mac Flecknoe (1682) is our first notable example. It tells how
Flecknoe, a contemporary poetaster, nominates Shadwell to suc-
ceed him as absolute monarch of 'all the Realms of *Non-sense*'; and
it describes Shadwell's coronation. Dryden's quarrel with Shadwell had several aspects, but literary differences dominate *Mac
Flecknoe*. The poem opens splendidly:

All humane things are subject to decay,
And, when Fate summons, Monarchs must obey:
This *Fleckno* found, who, like *Augustus*, young
Was call'd to Empire, and had govern'd long:
In Prose and Verse, was own'd, without dispute
Through all the Realms of *Non-sense*, absolute.
This aged Prince now flourishing in Peace,
And blest with issue of a large increase,
Worn out with business, did at length debate
To settle the succession of the State.

(ll. 1-10)

After a lofty general statement of the necessity which compels

Flecknoe, these lines ironically celebrate his long and peaceful reign and his numerous progeny before pointedly, and alliteratively, formulating the problem he has to face. He solves it by naming Shadwell:

> Some Beams of Wit on other souls may fall,
> Strike through and make a lucid intervall;
> But *Sh*—'s genuine night admits no ray,
> His rising Fogs prevail upon the Day:
> Besides his goodly Fabrick fills the eye,
> And seems design'd for thoughtless Majesty:
> Thoughtless as Monarch Oakes, that shade the plain,
> And, spread in solemn state, supinely reign.

(ll. 21–8)

This comes from the first of the two set speeches by the 'aged Prince' which make up the greater part of the poem. Though *Mac Flecknoe* does not quite live up to its magnificent opening, the mock-epic tone is successfully maintained to the end, when a farcical calamity terminates the action.

Mac Flecknoe gave Pope the central idea for *The Dunciad* (1728–43). In the original version of this, Lewis Theobald, the editor of Shakespeare, succeeded to the throne of Dullness; but when Pope revised the work Colley Cibber, the actor, playwright, and Poet Laureate, became the favoured candidate.

The Dunciad is a longer and more elaborate mock-epic than *Mac Flecknoe*. In conformity with ancient example, it starts with a proposition and an invocation; and a prayer and sacrifice to the goddess, her appearance and prophecy, and an acclamation of the hero follow before the end of Book i. In the remaining three books, the programme of 'high heroic Games' (ii. 18), the descent to 'th' Elysian Shade' (iii. 14), and the vision of future glories likewise parallel episodes occurring in one or more of the *Iliad*, the *Odyssey*, and the *Aeneid*. Pope's verse, too, brings the classical epics to mind, often by directly echoing them. From this point of view the most notable deficiency of *The Dunciad* is the slightness of its action. What sufficed for *Mac Flecknoe* proves inadequate for a work eight times as long.

Nevertheless, *The Dunciad* has an extraordinary power. This makes itself felt, for example, in the first glimpse of Cibber:

> Swearing and supperless the Hero sate,
> Blasphem'd his Gods, the Dice, and damn'd his Fate.
> Then gnaw'd his pen, then dash'd it on the ground,
> Sinking from thought to thought, a vast profound!
> Plung'd for his sense, but found no bottom there,
> Yet wrote and flounder'd on, in mere despair;
>
> (i. 115–20)

and it overwhelms us in the final apocalyptic vision of the triumph of Dullness:

> In vain, in vain, – the all-composing Hour
> Resistless falls: The Muse obeys the Pow'r.
> She comes! she comes! the sable Throne behold
> Of *Night* Primæval, and of *Chaos* old!
> Before her, *Fancy*'s gilded clouds decay,
> And all its varying Rain-bows die away.
> *Wit* shoots in vain its momentary fires,
> The meteor drops, and in a flash expires.
> As one by one, at dread Medea's strain,
> The sick'ning stars fade off th'ethereal plain;
> As Argus' eyes by Hermes' wand opprest,
> Clos'd one by one to everlasting rest;
> Thus at her felt approach, and secret might,
> *Art* after *Art* goes out, and all is Night.
> See skulking *Truth* to her old Cavern fled,
> Mountains of Casuistry heap'd o'er her head!
> *Philosophy*, that lean'd on Heav'n before,
> Shrinks to her second cause, and is no more.
> *Physic* of *Metaphysic* begs defence,
> And *Metaphysic* calls for aid on *Sense!*

See *Mystery* to *Mathematics* fly!
In vain! they gaze, turn giddy, rave, and die.
Religion blushing veils her sacred fires,
And unawares *Morality* expires.
Nor *public* Flame, nor *private*, dares to shine;
Nor *human* Spark is left, nor Glimpse *divine!*
Lo! thy dread Empire, CHAOS! is restor'd;
Light dies before thy uncreating word:
Thy hand, great Anarch! lets the curtain fall;
And Universal Darkness buries All.

(iv. 627–56)

Such passages as this testify to Pope's deep concern at what he believed to be a decline in standards of intelligence and taste. Other writers of mock-epics – Tassoni and Boileau, for example – have fun with the epic form. But in *The Dunciad* Pope feels such alarm at the way things are going that on the whole he neglects the amusement obtainable from comically belittling his model. Instead, he exploits the epic machinery and style almost solely to give force to his castigation of the corruptors by ironically exalting them. The result is one of the most urgent and impressive poems in the language, but one that many readers would prefer to call an epic satire rather than a mock-epic.

Pope's true mock-epic was *The Rape of the Lock* (1712–14). Tassoni, as we have seen, employed a bucket in the rôle of Helen of Troy; and Boileau made 'd'un vain Pupitre un second Ilion' (vi. 160; 'from a Simple *Desk* a Second *Iliad* fram'd' (tr. Ozell, 1708)). Pope, too, demonstrates 'What mighty Contests rise from trivial Things' (i. 2).

Robert, Lord Petre, had cut off a lock of Arabella Fermor's hair, and John Caryll had asked Pope to write a poem to heal the consequent estrangement between the two families. Seeking, in his own words, to 'laugh them together again', the poet resorted to the mock-epic. His *Rape of the Lock* is a beautifully balanced example of the *genre*. In it, he genially derides the traditional form by

using it for trivial affairs and at the same time emphasizes the triviality of those affairs by showing them to be unworthy of the form.

He starts in due style with a proposition and an invocation, and
his five short cantos contain an astonishing number of mock-
heroic allusions. Geoffrey Tillotson, in his Introduction to the
poem in the 'Twickenham Pope' (6 vols, London, 1939–61), shows
how he intensifies these by making most things 'smaller in size and
more femininely exquisite in quality' (p. 116). Thus, the hero is a
woman, the rape is that of a mere lock of hair, the epic feast becomes a coffee-party, the warrior's shield becomes a hoop petti-
coat, the deities include the minute and impalpable sylphs, and the
epic battles shrink to a game of cards and a hullabaloo in a draw-
ing-room. Even the Baron's prayer and sacrifice to the celestial
powers, and Umbriel's descent to the underworld, are accommo-
dated to this scale.

As a result, *The Rape of the Lock* is a mock-epic which wittily
and delicately re-creates the contemporary world to which it refers.
The classical epic poets make much of the arming of the hero for
battle. Pope's equivalent is the preparation of Belinda for en-
countering the social life of the day:

> And now, unveil'd, the *Toilet* stands display'd,
> Each Silver Vase in mystic Order laid.
> First, rob'd in White, the Nymph intent adores
> With Head uncover'd, the *Cosmetic* Pow'rs.
> A heav'nly Image in the Glass appears,
> To that she bends, to that her Eyes she rears;
> Th'inferior Priestess, at her Altar's side,
> Trembling, begins the sacred Rites of Pride.
> Unnumber'd Treasures ope at once, and here
> The various Off'rings of the World appear;
> From each she nicely culls with curious Toil,
> And decks the Goddess with the glitt'ring Spoil.
> This Casket *India*'s glowing Gems unlocks,
> And all *Arabia* breathes from yonder Box.

> The Tortoise here and Elephant unite,
> Transform'd to *Combs*, the speckled and the white.
> Here Files of Pins extend their shining Rows,
> Puffs, Powders, Patches, Bibles, Billet-doux.
> Now awful Beauty puts on all its Arms;
> The Fair each moment rises in her Charms,
> Repairs her Smiles, awakens ev'ry Grace,
> And calls forth all the Wonders of her Face;
> Sees by Degrees a purer Blush arise,
> And keener Lightnings quicken in her Eyes.
> The busy *Sylphs* surround their darling Care;
> These set the Head, and those divide the Hair,
> Some fold the Sleeve, whilst others plait the Gown;
> And *Betty*'s prais'd for Labours not her own.
>
> (i. 121–48)

The opening lines of this passage mockingly imply that the ritual possesses a religious significance; the articles displayed on the toilet-table sound almost like rarities in a royal treasury, though the incongruous 'Bibles' makes a satirical point in the culminating, alliterative line; rhetorical figures throughout dignify the proceedings; and the account of the supernatural attention lavished upon Belinda prepares for the deliberate anticlimax of the final clause.

The passage is characteristic of much that is finest in *The Rape of the Lock*. When Pope describes Hampton Court, where the Baron is to commit his crime, he delights in pointing out, with the help of two memorable instances of zeugma, how private concerns press on those who take responsibility for public affairs; and how the most trivial, if elegant, vanities can practically monopolize the thoughts of 'the Heroes and the Nymphs' with whom he is immediately concerned:

> Close by those Meads for ever crown'd with Flow'rs,
> Where *Thames* with Pride surveys his rising Tow'rs,
> There stands a Structure of Majestick Frame,
> Which from the neighb'ring *Hampton* takes its Name.

Here *Britain*'s Statesmen oft the Fall foredoom
Of Foreign Tyrants, and of Nymphs at home;
Here Thou, Great *Anna*! whom three Realms obey,
Dost sometimes Counsel take – and sometimes *Tea*.
  Hither the Heroes and the Nymphs resort,
To taste awhile the Pleasures of a Court;
In various Talk th'instructive hours they past,
Who gave the *Ball*, or paid the *Visit* last:
One speaks the Glory of the *British Queen*,
And one describes a charming *Indian Screen*;
A third interprets Motions, Looks, and Eyes;
At ev'ry Word a Reputation dies.
Snuff, or the *Fan*, supply each Pause of Chat,
With singing, laughing, ogling, and all that.

(iii. 1–18)

When Belinda finally meets the Baron in battle, Pope entertains
us with a narrative that simultaneously burlesques the martial
encounters of classical epic and exposes the triviality of the contemporary squabble:

See fierce *Belinda* on the *Baron* flies,
With more than usual Lightning in her Eyes;
Nor fear'd the Chief th'unequal Fight to try,
Who sought no more than on his Foe to die.
But this bold Lord, with manly Strength indu'd,
She with one Finger and a Thumb subdu'd:
Just where the Breath of Life his Nostrils drew,
A Charge of *Snuff* the wily Virgin threw;
The *Gnomes* direct, to ev'ry Atome just,
The pungent Grains of titillating Dust.
Sudden, with starting Tears each Eye o'erflows,
And the high Dome re-ecchoes to his Nose.

(v. 75–86)

Pope must have wondered what to do with the lock at the end
of the poem, just as Byron must have wondered what to do with
George III at the end of *The Vision of Judgment*. Its retention by

the Baron would be unjust, but its restoration to Belinda would be futile. Pope's happy solution came from a poem which had been a favourite since childhood. 'Ovid had ended his *Metamorphoses* by transforming the soul of Julius Caesar into a star. Callimachus had so transformed the locks of Berenice. Pope combines the two' (Tillotson, p. 116). In this way he brings to an apt conclusion the most delightful mock-poem in the language.

The mock-epic is not the only possible kind of mock-poem. We need feel no surprise that it has been the most important kind. Mockery naturally directs itself towards what is elevated, and the epic has commonly been thought the most elevated form of non-dramatic poetry. But less elevated forms can also attract mockery. I have mentioned that mock-lyric occurs incidentally in *Hudibras*; *Sir Thopas*, the tale supposedly told by Chaucer himself to the Canterbury pilgrims, is an entertaining mock-romance; and Cowper's 'Diverting History of John Gilpin' is a lively mock-ballad.

Pastoral, too, has invited mock-poetic treatment. As normally practised in the tradition stemming from Virgil's imitations of Theocritus, pastoral gives elaborately conventional expression to an urban writer's longing for the peace and simplicity of rural existence. Its idealized shepherds and shepherdesses adopt elegant poses as singers, as lovers, or as mourners.

In *The Shepherd's Week* (1714), John Gay, the friend of Pope, writes of shepherds and shepherdesses more realistically and more humorously than this. His characters bear such names as Marian, Susan, Cuddy, and Lobbin Clout; they refer to the occupations, customs and beliefs, and occasionally use the colloquial and dialect words, of the English countrypeople of their time; and the situations in which they find themselves can be distinctly ludicrous. At the same time, Gay does not forget that he is writing a sort of pastoral. Each of the six poems in his series deals with one of the conventional themes: two shepherds compete in song, for example, or a forsaken girl bewails her fate, or two men mourn the dead woman whom both loved. Metrically and syntactically, Gay preserves a correct pastoral tone, even though his diction sometimes qualifies it. Many of his proper names are facetiously elevated above the words from which they patently derive; instances include Blouzelinda, Clumsilis, Grubbinol, Hobnelia, and Bowzybeus. One shepherd sings,

> Leek to the *Welch*, to *Dutchmen* butter's dear,
> Of *Irish* swains potatoe is the chear;
> Oats for their feasts the *Scottish* shepherds grind,
> Sweet turnips are the food of *Blouzelind*.
> While she loves turnips, butter I'll despise,
> Nor leeks nor oatmeal nor potatoe prize.

His companion responds,

> In good roast-beef my landlord sticks his knife,
> The capon fat delights his dainty wife,
> Pudding our Parson eats, the Squire loves hare,
> But white-pot thick is my *Buxoma*'s fare.
> While she loves white-pot, capon ne'er shall be,
> Nor hare, nor beef, nor pudding, food for me.
>
> ('Monday; or, The Squabble', ll. 83–94)

We smile at the combination of pastoral rhetoric with commonplace fact. But Grubbinol's lament for the dead Blouzelinda gives particularity to a collective grief:

> To her sweet mem'ry, flow'ry garlands strung,
> O'er her now empty seat aloft were hung.
> With wicker rods we fenc'd her tomb around,
> To ward from man and beast the hallow'd ground,
> Lest her new grave the Parson's cattle raze,
> For both his horse and cow the church-yard graze.
>   Now we trudg'd homeward to her mother's farm,
> To drink new cyder mull'd, with ginger warm.

For gaffer *Tread-well* told us by the by,
Excessive sorrow is exceeding dry.
   While bulls bear horns upon their curled brow,
Or lasses with soft stroakings milk the cow;
While padling ducks the standing lake desire,
Or batt'ning hogs roll in the sinking mire;
While moles the crumbled earth in hillocks raise,
So long shall swains tell *Blouʒelinda*'s praise.

This is not the end of the story, however. Grubbinol and Bum-kinet conclude their laments.

   Thus wail'd the louts in melancholy strain,
'Till bonny *Susan* sped a-cross the plain;
They seiz'd the lass in apron clean array'd,
And to the ale-house forc'd the willing maid;
In ale and kisses they forget their cares,
And *Susan Blouʒelinda*'s loss repairs.

                              ('Friday; or, The Dirge', ll. 143–64)

'Wednesday; or, The Dumps' and 'Thursday; or, The Spell' end equally humorously.

We must not over-simplify Gay's achievement. On the one hand, his employment of the pastoral form makes us acutely conscious of the clumsiness and grossness of his rustics; on the other hand, his persons are so down-to-earth that we cannot avoid recognizing the affectations and pretences of the pastoral form. For our present purposes, he is a writer of mock-pastoral; but we do him less than justice if we do not perceive that he is also pointing forward to the seriously realistic presentation of rural subjects.

The fact that so many of the finest mock-poems belong to the century following the appearance of *Le Lutrin* should cause no surprise. This period saw the widest acceptance of the neo-classical view that the various *genres* or kinds of poetry are as distinct from one another as are the biological species, and that an appropriate set of rules can be framed for compositions in each. As long as the kinds were firmly established, mock-kinds could flourish. But the Romantics rejected the doctrine of kinds and the rules associated with it. They held that each true poem evolves, in accordance with organic laws, into its own unique final form. Instead of poems that belong to kinds, they created individual poems. As a result, parody displaced the mock-poem as the principal mode of high burlesque.

Nevertheless, fashions in taste have occasionally resulted in the temporary emergence of literary kinds even during the past two centuries, and when this has happened a corresponding mock-kind has become possible. In so far as it burlesques the primitivist novel in general, Stella Gibbons' *Cold Comfort Farm*, as we have seen, realizes this possibility. On the whole, however, the nearest we get to the mock-poem in the present century is in the burlesque of the mental habits and the jargon of particular trades, professions, and other social groups. When Paul Jennings writes a piece of spoof Higher Journalism on the modish French philosophy 'Resistentialism', or Daniel Bell concocts 'The Parameters of Social Movements: A Formal Paradigm' with so straight a face that fellow-sociologists fail to appreciate that he is joking, we have perhaps the mock-poems of our own age. Dwight Macdonald prints both of these in his excellent anthology.

6

Dramatic Burlesque

One of the best-known dramatic burlesques in the English language is the short play of Pyramus and Thisbe performed by Nick Bottom and his companions in *A Midsummer Night's Dream* (about 1595). Shakespeare was ridiculing the interludes of the previous generation, but readers and theatre-goers who know nothing of these still find the piece irresistibly funny.

A dozen or so years later, Francis Beaumont produced one of our earliest full-length dramatic burlesques. His *Knight of the Burning Pestle* (1607) exploits the device of having actors masquerade as members of the audience. A supposed Citizen and Wife, George and Nell, protest against the Prologue's announcement of a play called *The London Merchant*. Suspecting that this will contain gibes at citizens, they insist on the insertion into the performance of a second plot in which a grocer, a member of George's own trade, will shine as a gallant knight-errant. They secure this rôle for their stage-struck apprentice Rafe, who has accompanied them to the theatre.

Remaining on stage throughout, they comment freely both upon the dramatic action and upon their fellow-spectators. So compelling do they find the theatrical illusion that they repeatedly mistake the fictional characters and situations for reality. This happens not only in connection with *The London Merchant* but also in connection with the plot of the knight-errant, despite the fact that they are themselves responsible for improvising it.

Their reactions to the performance show them to be a very characteristic middle-aged pair from the shopkeeping class of early seventeenth-century London. They resent the effrontery of the apprentice Jasper in presuming to love his master's daughter; they wish to see her united with Humphrey, the rival favoured by her father. Humphrey prompts maternal feelings in the Wife, and when Jasper beats him she intervenes with practical consolation – 'some greene ginger' (II. v) – and prudent advice to invoke the law. Though the Citizen sees Jasper's handiness with his fists as a sign of grace in one whom in general he condemns, he joins his Wife in demanding that the knight-errant chastise Jasper. To their chagrin, Jasper chastises Rafe. They bring consolation – 'some suger-candy' (II. vii), this time – and advice to this new victim. When Jasper conducts his absurd test of Luce by pretending to be about to kill her, Nell calls on George in terror to 'raise the watch at *Ludgate*' (III. i); and, when the knight-errant has spent a night at an inn, Nell inquires whether he slept well, and George foots the bill. Nell offers her homely remedies for chilblains to one of the characters. Entertaining high hopes for Rafe as the Knight of the Burning Pestle, she and her husband require the deferment of an item of *London Merchant* business. In short, they are imposing their own fancies and desires upon a pattern of illusions created for their entertainment and then mistaking the whole sequence for reality.

Much about *The London Merchant* was designed to please them. It is a play about London life in their own social class, with pointed contrasts between prudence and prodigality and with a well-developed love-story. Yet their original suspicion of it was not altogether unjustified. The presumptuous apprentice Jasper finally wins his master's daughter; and Merrythought, Jasper's idle, roistering father, finally triumphs over his thrifty wife. George and Nell, sharing the mercenary values of Luce's father and Mistress Merrythought, must have felt that the familiar material was being used to point a very dangerous moral.

Nor does the subversiveness of *The London Merchant* end there. Though the Citizen and his Wife take it all quite guilelessly, the play burlesques a kind of drama much favoured by people like themselves. The burlesque is most obvious in Humphrey's speeches, where rhyme emphasizes it:

> for love hath tost me,
> In furious blanket like a Tennis ball,
> And now I rise aloft, and now I fall.
>
> (I. ii)

Admittedly, Humphrey is a fool, and his speeches characterize him as such. But his foolishness so completely disqualifies him in our eyes as a contender with Jasper for the hand of Luce that we can hardly take the lovers' difficulties seriously. The heavy father is ludicrously explicit to Jasper:

> As I remember, you had never charge,
> To love your Maisters daughter, and even then,
> When I had found a wealthy husband for her;
>
> (I. i)

and the flight of the lovers takes them no farther than Waltham, or Epping, Forest, which then began just outside the northern gates of the city.

In 'this wilde un-peopled place', Jasper resolves to test Luce:

> Though certainely I am certaine of her love,
> I'le try her, that the world and memory
> May sing to after times, her constancie.
>
> (III. i)

This is the kind of tired theatrical cliché that invites burlesque treatment: it is one of several that Beaumont exploits. A coffin containing the reputedly dead Jasper is carried into the room where Luce's father has confined her. Luce has a long speech of mourning, and there follows a melancholy song. Then she declares,

> Thou sable cloth, sad cover of my joies
> I lift thee up, and thus I meete with death,

and Jasper, sitting up in the coffin, retorts, 'And thus you meete the living' (IV. iv). A final example occurs when Jasper, with '*his face mealed*', pretends to be his own ghost and terrifies Luce's father in the midst of his preparations for marrying her to Humphrey: 'Forbeare thy paines fond man, it is too late.' He instructs him to 'beat fond *Humphrey* out of thy dores', and Nell, remembering Rafe's suffering, exclaims with an incongruous sense of outrage: 'Looke *George*, his very Ghost would have folkes beaten' (V. i).

In all this, however, the burlesque is less extravagant than in the plot of the knight-errant. This shows Rafe as a kind of Don Quixote. Beaumont probably had no first-hand knowledge of Cervantes' great burlesque of the romances of chivalry, which did not appear in English until 1612; but he must have known about it from hearsay. Like Don Quixote's, Rafe's head has been turned by the romantic tales to which he is addicted. He asks 'what brave spirit could be content to sit in his shop with a flappet of wood and a blew apron before him . . ., that might pursue feats of Armes, and through his noble atchievments procure . . . a famous history to be written of his heroicke prowesse'. He decides that 'my elder Prentice *Tim* shall be my trusty Squire, and little *George* my Dwarfe' and proceeds to put them through their paces, to the accompaniment of a commentary from the Citizen and his Wife:

> RAFE. My beloved Squire *Tim*, stand out, admit this were a Desart, and over it a Knight errant pricking, and I should bid you inquire of his intents, what would you say?
>
> SQUIRE. Sir, my Maister sent me, to know whether [i.e., whither] you are riding?
>
> RAFE. No, thus; faire sir, the *Right Courteous and Valiant Knight of the burning Pestle*, commanded me to enquire, upon what adventure you are bound, whether to relieve some distressed Damsels, or otherwise.
>
> CITIZEN. Whoresonne blocke-head cannot remember.

E

WIFE. I'faith, and *Rafe* told him on't before, all the Gentlemen [i.e., her fellow-spectators] heard him, did he not Gentlemen, did not *Rafe* tel him on't?

DWARFE. *Right Courteous and Valiant Knight of the burning Pestle*, here is a distressed Damsell, to have a halfe penny-worth of pepper.

WIFE. That's a good boy, see, the little boy can hit it, by my troth it's a fine child.

RAFE. Relieve her with all courteous language, now shut up shoppe, no more my Prentices, but my trusty Squire and Dwarfe.

(I. iii)

His first quest, for the lost property of Mistress Merrythought, brings him to the Bell Inn at Waltham, which he mistakes in truly quixotic style. To the Tapster's words of welcome, he replies:

Faire Squire *Tapstero*, I a wandring Knight,
Hight of the burning Pestle, in the quest
Of this faire Ladies Casket, and wrought
   [i.e., embroidered] purse,
Loosing my selfe in this vast Wildernesse
Am to this Castle well by fortune brought,
Where hearing of the goodly entertaine
Your Knight of holy Order of the *Bell*
Gives to all Damsels, and all errant Knights,
I thought to knocke, and now am bold to enter.

(II. vii)

In the same style, he mistakes a barber–surgeon and his patients for the giant Barbaroso and his prisoners. He liberates the patients.

Rafe in his fictional rôle is thus the means by which Beaumont burlesques the popular romances of chivalry. While burlesquing one popular kind of drama in *The London Merchant*, he burlesques a second through the sequence of disconnected adventures which the Citizen and his Wife devise for their apprentice. When they demand that Pompiona, daughter of the King of Moldavia, fall in love with Rafe, they are told that 'it will shew ill-favouredly to have a Grocers prentice to court a kings daughter'. George is indignant.

> Will it so sir? you are well read in Histories: I pray you what was sir *Dagonet?* was not he prentice to a Grocer in London? read the play of the *Foure Prentices of London*, where they tosse their pikes so: I pray you fetch him in sir, fetch him in.
>
> (IV. i)

They have their way. Subsequent demands result in the appearance of Rafe as Lord of the May, as an officer of the London militia, and as a mortally wounded hero.

The play which George cites, Thomas Heywood's *Four Prentices of London*, exemplifies the second kind of drama Beaumont was burlesquing. It links the most extravagant adventures with the most extravagant adulation of the city.

In deriding the sub-culture of the London shopkeepers of his time, Beaumont was evidently catering for a sophisticated audience. He ridicules the attitudes and values of his victims by means of the direct satirical representation of the Citizen and his Wife. He ridicules their tastes by means of the two mock-plays, *The London Merchant* and the plot of the knight-errant. In these he burlesques respectively the domestic drama and the adventure drama as composed for citizen audiences; and in Rafe's infatuation with tales of chivalry he burlesques, often by parody, one of the citizens' favourite forms of reading. Neither his direct satire nor his burlesque is really harsh. Perhaps his original audience would have preferred something less goodnatured. Whatever the explanation, *The Knight of the Burning Pestle* failed when first staged.

The Restoration period, which saw the rapid development in England of the travesty, the Hudibrastic, and the mock-poem, saw the establishment also of a tradition of dramatic burlesque which was to flourish for two centuries and more. A dramatic burlesque tends to be centrally a mock-play, and therefore a variety of mock-poem in the sense in which I have been using this term. But, just as *The Knight of the Burning Pestle* includes also direct satire and parody, so do many later instances combine several different methods of attack.

The finest dramatic burlesque of the Restoration period is *The Rehearsal* (produced 1671, printed 1672), by George Villiers, second Duke of Buckingham. This ridicules the heroic drama of the age. Dryden described an heroic play as an imitation of an epic on a small scale. It normally had a warrior-hero, an action on which the fate of an empire depended, and an elevated style. Under the influence of French tragedy, English authors often chose to write in rhyming couplets; and they commonly based their plots on a conflict between love and honour. Dryden himself wrote the most successful examples, so he naturally became Buckingham's principal victim. He took his revenge nine years later when he portrayed Buckingham as Zimri, the unstable playboy politician, in *Absalom and Achitophel*, i.

Whereas Beaumont shows his mock-plays in performance, Buckingham shows his mock-play in rehearsal. Its author, Mr Bayes, instructs the actors and explains his work to two acquaintances. He is conceited and opinionated and, in the form in which we have *The Rehearsal*, evidently represents Dryden. But there may well have been an earlier draft in which Dryden was not the chief butt; and even in the published version the characterization glances at other authors of heroic plays as well as the Poet Laureate.

The plot of the mock-play consists of a haphazard sequence of situations taken from the heroic drama. Bayes asks at one point, 'why, what a Devil is the Plot good for, but to bring in fine things?' (III. i). Without assenting to his view in general, we may certainly agree that the plot which starts with the dethronement of the two Kings of Brentford, continues with a series of pointless surprises, and breaks off with the military triumph of the fierce Drawcansir, enables Buckingham to bring in a prodigious

number of parodies. The dialogue of his mock-play contains little
else.

Drawcansir fulminates in the manner of Dryden's Almanzor in
The Conquest of Granada:

> Others may bost a single man to kill;
> But I, the blood of thousands daily spill.
> Let petty Kings the names of Parties know:
> Where e'er I come, I slay both friend and foe.
> The swiftest Horsmen my swift rage controuls,
> And from their Bodies drives their trembling souls.
> If they had wings, and to the Gods could flie,
> I would pursue and beat 'em through the skie:
> And make proud *Jove*, with all his Thunder, see
> This single Arm more dreadful is, than he.

(V. i)

Prince Volscius, who falls in love while pulling on his boots, finds
in his legs, one booted and the other not, an emblem of the conflict
between love and honour which agitates him:

> How has my passion Made me *Cupid's* scoff!
> This hasty Boot is on, the other off,
> And sullen lies, with amorous design
> To quit loud fame, and make that Beauty mine. . . .
> My Legs, the Emblem of my various thought,
> Shew to what sad distraction I am brought.
> Sometimes with stubborn Honour, like this Boot,
> My mind is guarded, and resolv'd: to do't:
> Sometimes, again, that very mind, by Love
> Disarmed, like this other Leg does prove.
> Shall I to Honour or to Love give way?
> Go on, cries Honour; tender Love saies, nay:
> Honour, aloud, commands, pluck both Boots on;
> But softer Love does whisper put on none.
> What shall I do? what conduct shall I find
> To lead me through this twy-light of my mind?

> For as bright Day with black approach of Night
> Contending, makes a doubtful puzling light;
> So does my Honour and my Love together
> Puzzle me so, I can resolve for neither.
> [*Goes out hopping with one Boot on, and the other off.*

(III. v)

With characteristic self-satisfaction, Bayes claims that he has made

one of the most delicate dainty *Simile's* in the whole world, I gad, if I
knew but how to applie it . . . 'Tis an allusion to love.

> So Boar and Sow, when any storm is nigh,
> Snuff up, and smell it gath'ring in the sky;
> Boar beckons Sow to trot in Chestnut Groves,
> And there consummate their unfinish'd Loves:
> Pensive in mud they wallow all alone,
> And snore and gruntle to each others moan.

(I. ii)

This parodies a simile in the second part of Dryden's *Conquest of Granada*:

> So, two kind turtles, when a storm is nigh,
> Look up, and see it gathering in the sky:
> Each calls his mate, to shelter in the groves,
> Leaving, in murmur, their unfinished loves:
> Perched on some drooping branch, they sit alone,
> And coo, and hearken to each other's moan.

(I. ii)

Less genial than *The Knight of the Burning Pestle*, *The Rehearsal* achieves its own kind of success. By the satirical presentation of Bayes, and by his mock-play with its ramshackle plot and grotesque parodies, it delivers an apt criticism of the heroic dramatists' striving for novelty, grandeur, and sensation.

In *The Tragedy of Tragedies; or, The Life and Death of Tom Thumb the Great* (1731), Henry Fielding dispenses with the machinery of fictional performance or rehearsal. He leaves his mock-play to speak for itself on the stage, though he associates a burlesque editorial apparatus of preface and notes with the printed text. Necessarily, its plot is more coherent, though no less absurd, than that of Bayes' piece about the dethronement and restoration of the two Kings of Brentford.

Tom Thumb opens immediately after its hero has defeated the giants. Its principal characters fall in love at cross-purposes. Tom Thumb loves King Arthur's daughter, Huncamunca, and is loved by his captive giantess, Glumdalca. While the King loves Glumdalca, his wife, Queen Dollallolla, loves Tom, who has a rival for the love of Huncamunca in Lord Grizzle. Huncamunca loves Tom and Grizzle equally. When she marries Tom, Grizzle leads a rebellion. He enters, proclaiming:

> Thus far our Arms with Victory are crown'd;
> For tho' we have not fought, yet we have found
> No enemy to fight withal.
>
> (III. vii)

Tom defeats and slays him. On receiving the news, the court begins to celebrate; the King orders the release of prisoners and the payment of their debts. But a messenger arrives:

> *Noodle.* Oh! monstrous, dreadful, terrible, Oh! Oh!
> Deaf be my Ears, for ever blind, my Eyes!
> Dumb be my Tongue! Feet lame! All Senses lost!
> Howl Wolves, grunt Bears, hiss Snakes, shriek all ye Ghosts!
>   *King.* What does the Blockhead mean?
>   *Noodle.* I mean, my Liege
> Only to grace my Tale with decent Horror;
> Whilst from my Garret, twice two Stories high,
> I look'd abroad into the Streets below;
> I saw *Tom Thumb* attended by the Mob,
> Twice Twenty Shoe-Boys, twice two Dozen Links,
> Chairmen and Porters, Hackney-Coachmen, Whores;

> Aloft he bore the grizly Head of *Grizzle*;
> When of a sudden thro' the Streets there came
> A Cow, of larger than the usual Size,
> And in a Moment – guess, Oh! guess the rest!
> And in a Moment swallow'd up *Tom Thumb*.
>> *King.* Shut up again the Prisons, bid my Treasurer
> Not give three Farthings out – hang all the *Culprits*,
> Guilty or not – no matter – Ravish Virgins,
> Go bid the Schoolmasters whip all their Boys;
> Let Lawyers, Parsons, and Physicians loose,
> To rob, impose on, and to kill the World.

(III. x)

This is typical of Fielding's tone and method. The main object of his attack, as of Buckingham's, is the heroic drama. Although most serious playwrights had stopped using rhyme after 1678, and although few were any longer writing in the heroic manner in 1731 even in blank verse, the old heroic plays still enjoyed great popularity on the stage. Fielding applies their rhetoric and bombast to the homely story of a diminutive folk-hero. The speeches I have cited exemplify the resultant incongruity between style and subject.

In footnotes to these speeches, Fielding's supposed editor draws attention to the fact that the 'beautiful Phrases' in Noodle's fourth line 'are all to be found in one single Speech of *King Arthur*, or *The British Worthy*' and that his fifth and sixth lines resemble two from Dryden's *Cleomenes*:

> I was but teaching him to grace his Tale
> With decent Horror.

Having maintained in his preface that *Tom Thumb* 'was written in the Reign of Queen *Elizabeth*', the editor has to assume that the writers whose phrases Fielding has borrowed or parodied were in fact the plagiarists. Again and again he says so: 'This Speech hath been taken to pieces by several Tragical Authors who seem to have rifled it and shared its Beauties among them', for example, and

'There is not one Beauty in this Charming Speech, but hath been borrowed by almost every Tragick Writer' (I. iii). Such notes naturally, and conveniently, list the phrases which Fielding has judged absurd enough to contribute to his characters' stilted orations. Grizzle's rhapsody to Huncamunca is ludicrous in itself:

> Oh! *Huncamunca, Huncamunca*, oh!
> Thy pouting Breasts, like Kettle-Drums of Brass,
> Beat everlasting loud Alarms of Joy;
> As bright as Brass they are, and oh, as hard;
> Oh *Huncamunca, Huncamunca*! oh!
>
> (II. v)

But the editor's note adds to our enjoyment by revealing that Fielding is echoing James Thomson: 'This beautiful Line, which ought, says Mr. W— to be written in Gold, is imitated in the New *Sophonisba*;

> Oh! *Sophonisba, Sophonisba,* oh!'

Thomson's infamous line also prompted a theatre-goer to call out from the pit, 'O, Jemmy Thomson, Jemmy Thomson, O!'

The supposed editor of *Tom Thumb* does not limit himself to recording parallel passages. A solemn pedant, he comments, interprets, investigates allusions, and evaluates conjectural emendations. His antics, a burlesque of scholarship, serve as a foil to the play itself, a burlesque of heroic tragedy.

Tom Thumb's similes call for a word in conclusion. Epic similes had naturally been frequent in heroic drama, and subsequent playwrights remained fond of ending scenes or acts with them. Fielding, mimicking this practice, develops explicit comparisons in choice language and elaborate syntax. But he invariably selects a commonplace vehicle that will clash not only with the style in which it is conveyed but also with the lofty tenor it purports to serve. A good example occurs at the end of Act II. Huncamunca,

F

in love simultaneously with Grizzle and Tom Thumb, sees that
she is in danger of losing both:

> I, who this Morn, of two chose which to wed,
> May go again this Night alone to Bed;
> So have I seen some wild unsettled Fool,
> Who had her Choice of this, and that Joint Stool;
> To give the Preference to either, loath
> And fondly coveting to sit on both:
> While the two Stools her Sitting Part confound,
> Between 'em both fall Squat upon the Ground.

Much dramatic burlesque dates from this period. Gay's *Beggar's
Opera* (1728) was in part a burlesque of the popular Italian opera;
and in 1734, four years after the staging of *Tom Thumb* in its
original, unexpanded form, Henry Carey, already a successful
parodist, produced the burlesque *Chrononhotonthologos: The Most
Tragical Tragedy, That ever was Tragediʒ'd by any Company of
Tragedians*. His 'Prologue' promises ridicule of the '*big bellowing
Bombast*' of modern poetasters. The play opens with Chrononhotonthologos seeking rest:

> Fatigu'd with the tremendous Toils of War,
> Within his Tent, on downy Couch succumbent,
> Himself he unfatigues with gentle Slumbers;

and shortly before its close his murderer cries out for the means of
bringing a doctor:

> Ha! What have I done?
> Go, call a Coach, and let a Coach be call'd;
> And let the Man that calls it be the Caller;
> And, in his Calling, let him nothing call,
> But Coach! Coach! Coach! Oh! for a Coach, ye Gods!

Carey does not maintain this level throughout. But his play has
other moments as happy as these.

The friend who wrote the 'Prologue' to Sheridan's *The Critic* observed that whereas in the age of Dryden

> The Tragick Queen, to please a tasteless crow'd,
> Had learn'd to bellow, rant, and roar so loud,
> That frighten'd Nature, her best friend before,
> The blust'ring beldam's company forswore . . .
> In our more pious, and far chaster times!
> These sure no longer are the Muse's crimes! . . .
> The frantick hero's wild delirium past,
> Now insipidity succeeds bombast.

Insipid and sentimental tragedies were certainly enjoying considerable favour. At the same time, the military triumphs of the early and middle years of the eighteenth century had created a lively demand for plays and spectacles based on English history. *The Critic*, first staged in 1779 and printed in 1781 while the army was suffering reverses at the hands of the American colonists, burlesques these contemporary trends. It contains very little parody. Even the passages which recall Shakespeare are evidently intended, not to parody him, but to burlesque the current fashion for imitating him.

Sheridan follows Buckingham in showing his mock-play in rehearsal. Act I introduces its author, Puff, and his friends, the gullible Dangle and the sarcastic Sneer. In Acts II and III they attend a rehearsal of as much of Puff's play as has survived the actors' ruthless cuts. Puff takes an early opportunity of declaring that

> when history, and particularly the history of our own country, furnishes any thing like a case in point, to the time in which an author writes, if he knows his own interest he will take advantage of it; so, Sir, I call my tragedy THE SPANISH ARMADA; and have laid the scene before TILBURY FORT.

> (II. i)

Mrs Dangle has already voiced fears of a French invasion. Since there seemed to be grounds for these at the time, Puff can regard the attempted Spanish invasion as 'a case in point'.

The mock-play opens in II. ii with Sir Christopher Hatton asking Sir Walter Raleigh the reason for the military preparations going on around them. 'Pray, Mr. Puff,' asks Sneer, 'how came Sir Christopher Hatton never to ask that question before?' 'What, before the Play began?' retorts Puff, 'how the plague could he?' The impressionable Dangle comments, 'That's true efaith!' Eventually Sir Christopher surmises that 'The state some danger apprehends!' 'A very cautious conjecture that', interjects Sneer.

Puff would seem to have embarked upon the common type of dramatic exposition in which an informant explains to an inquirer everything that the audience needs to know. But before long Sir Christopher is joining in the explanation:

> *Sir Walter.* PHILIP you know is proud, IBERIA's king!
> *Sir Christopher.* He is.
> *Sir Walter.* – His subjects in base bigotry
>   And Catholic oppression held, – while we
>   You know, the protestant persuasion hold.
> *Sir Christopher.* We do.
> *Sir Walter.* You know beside, – his boasted armament,
>   The fam'd Armada, – by the Pope baptized,
>   With purpose to invade these realms –
> *Sir Christopher.*   – Is sailed,
>   Our last advices so report.
> *Sir Walter.* While the Iberian Admiral's chief hope,
>   His darling son –
> *Sir Christopher.* Ferolo Whiskerandos hight –
> *Sir Walter.* The same – by chance a pris'ner hath been ta'en,
>   And in this fort of Tilbury –
> *Sir Christopher.*   – Is now
>   Confin'd, – 'tis true, and oft from yon tall turrets top
>   I've mark'd the youthful Spaniard's haughty mien
>   Unconquer'd, tho' in chains;
> *Sir Walter.*   You also know –

This is too much even for as receptive a playgoer as Dangle: 'Mr. Puff, as he *knows* all this, why does Sir Walter go on telling him?' Puff's reply is conclusive: 'But the audience are not supposed to know any thing of the matter, are they?'

Twice in the few lines quoted so far Sheridan has mocked the conventions that govern our understanding of the relationship between stage illusion and everyday reality: once when Puff explains why Sir Christopher has not asked his question before, and again when he asserts the over-riding obligation to inform the audience. A third instance occurs when Sneer finds an eaves-dropping incident implausible. 'O lud, Sir,' protests Puff, 'if people who want to listen, or overhear, were not always conniv'd at in a Tragedy, there would be no carrying on any plot in the world.' Throughout *The Critic*, as throughout *The Knight of the Burning Pestle*, this is an important theme of the burlesque.

Another important theme receives emphasis with the entry of the Earl of Leicester. His first speech could stand on its own as a delicate and accurate parody of Shakespeare:

> How's this my friends! is't thus your new fledg'd zeal
> And plumed valor moulds in roosted sloth?
> Why dimly glimmers that heroic flame,
> Whose red'ning blaze by patriot spirit fed,
> Should be the beacon of a kindling realm?
> Can the quick current of a patriot heart,
> Thus stagnate in a cold and weedy converse,
> Or freeze in tideless inactivity?
> No! rather let the fountain of your valor
> Spring thro' each stream of enterprise,
> Each petty channel of conducive daring,
> Till the full torrent of your foaming wrath
> O'erwhelm the flats of sunk hostility!

In its context, however, this forms part of Sheridan's burlesque of the neo-Shakespeareans of his own time. Leicester's rebuke stimulates the patriotism of the others. They all take hands as Sir Walter voices their determination:

> in friendship's closing line
> We'll grapple with despair, and if we fall,
> We'll fall in Glory's wake!

Leicester. There spoke Old England's genius!
   Then, are we all resolv'd?
All. We are – all resolv'd!
Leicester. To conquer – or be free?
All. To conquer, or be free!
Leicester. All?
All. All!

'*Nem. con.* egad!' observes the sardonic Sneer. 'O yes,' replies Puff, 'where they *do* agree on the stage, their unanimity is wonderful!'

This seems to be the earliest example in English dramatic burlesque of the joke against patriotism. Sheridan develops it. When Leicester and the others have sworn to 'conquer, or be free', apparently without noticing that these are not really alternatives, they sink upon their knees in prayer. The effect so delights Puff that for a moment he wishes the actors to 'go off kneeling'.

Nor does the burlesque of patriotism end here. In III. i, when five characters are threatening to use their swords and daggers on one another, a Beefeater charges them all to drop their weapons 'In the Queen's name'. The immediate clatter of ironmongery inevitably raises a laugh. Moreover, the mock-play ends with a patriotic spectacle. 'Now then', exclaims Puff, 'for my magnificence! – my battle! – my noise! – and my procession!' The stage direction reads:

> *Flourish of drums – trumpets – cannon, &c. &c. Scene changes to the sea – the fleets engage – the musick plays 'Britons strike home.' – Spanish fleet destroyed by fire-ships, &c. – English fleet advances – musick plays 'Rule Britannia.' – The procession of all the English rivers and their tributaries with their emblems, &c. begins with Handels water musick, ends with a chorus, to the march in Judas Maccabaeus.*

Naturally, *The Spanish Armada* has also its sentimental interest. Tilburina, the daughter of the Governor of the fort, has fallen in love with his prisoner, Don Ferolo Whiskerandos. Through her, the Spaniard tries to bribe the Governor to release him. Puff renders the Governor's struggle with his conscience in a dialogue with Tilburina in II. ii. This dialogue, he says, exemplifies the 'sort of small-sword logic, which we have borrowed from the French'.

Tilburina. A retreat in Spain!
Governor. Outlawry here!
Tilburina. Your daughter's prayer!
Governor. Your father's oath!
Tilburina. My lover!
Governor. My country!
Tilburina. Tilburina!
Governor. England!
Tilburina. A title!
Governor. Honor!
Tilburina. A pension!
Governor. Conscience!
Tilburina. A thousand pounds!
Governor. Hah! thou hast touch'd me nearly!

The Critic is the most precisely and elegantly absurd of all English dramatic burlesques. *The Knight of the Burning Pestle*, its strongest rival, is admittedly more robustly and broadly humorous; but *The Critic* surpasses it in sophisticated intelligence and in wit. The Beefeater's soliloquy and the silent Burleigh in III. i show it at its most hilariously entertaining. The Beefeater enters, saying, 'Perdition catch my soul but *I* do love thee.' When Dangle suspects that there is something like this in *Othello*, Puff dismisses the coincidence as fortuitous, and the actor supplies the other three lines of his soliloquy:

Beefeater. Tho' hopeless love finds comfort in despair,
   It never can endure a rival's bliss!
But soft – I am observ'd.   [*Exit* BEEFEATER.

Dangle. That's a very short soliloquy.

Puff. Yes – but it would have been a great deal longer if he had not been observed.

Sneer. A most sentimental Beefeater that, Mr. Puff.

Puff. Hearke – I would not have you be too sure that he *is* a Beef-eater.

Sneer. What a hero in disguise?

Puff. No matter – I only give you a hint – But now for my principal character – Here he comes – LORD BURLEIGH in person! Pray, gentlemen, step this way – softly – I only hope the Lord High Treasurer is perfect – if he is but perfect!

Enter BURLEIGH, *goes slowly to a chair and sits.*

Sneer. Mr. Puff!

Puff. Hush! vastly well, Sir! vastly well! a most interesting gravity!

Dangle. What, isn't he to speak at all?

Puff. Egad, I thought you'd ask me that – yes, it is a very likely thing – that a Minister in his situation, with the whole affairs of the nation on his head, should have time to talk! – but hush! or you'll put him out.

Sneer. Put him out! how the plague can that be, if he's not going to say any thing?

Puff. There's a reason! why his part is to *think*, and how the plague! do you imagine he can *think* if you keep talking?

Dangle. That's very true upon my word!

[BURLEIGH *comes forward, shakes his head, and exit.*

Sneer. He is very perfect, indeed – Now, pray what did he mean by that?

Puff. You don't take it?

Sneer. No; I don't upon my soul.

Puff. Why, by that shake of the head, he gave you to understand that even tho' they had more justice in their cause and wisdom in their measures – yet, if there was not a greater spirit shown on the part of the people – the country would at last fall a sacrifice to the hostile ambition of the Spanish monarchy.

Sneer. The devil! – did he mean all that by shaking his head?

Puff. Every word of it – If he shook his head as I taught him.

Later authors of successful dramatic burlesques have sometimes written with the reader, rather than the playgoer, in mind. George Canning, J. H. Frere, and George Ellis had no thought of performance when they ridiculed recent German drama in *The Rovers* (1798). Nor had Max Beerbohm when he burlesqued Elizabethan drama in *Savonarola Brown* (1919). Of the nineteenth-century examples intended for the theatre, the finest are perhaps the libretti of *Trial by Jury* (1875) and *H.M.S. Pinafore* (1878) by W. S. Gilbert. *H.M.S. Pinafore*, in particular, makes excellent entertainment out of the goodnatured mockery on the one hand of the generally accepted image of the navy and on the other of the conventions of opera. George Bernard Shaw brought the form into the twentieth century with *The Admirable Bashville* (1901), in which he amusingly mimics Elizabethan blank verse.

Although distinguished achievements were rare, dramatic burlesques enjoyed great popularity on the nineteenth-century stage. Early and mid-Victorian audiences evidently preferred low to high burlesque. Not only travesty but also the low burlesque of more general application – that which in earlier centuries had manifested itself as Hudibrastic – delighted them. The works in question were too trivial to be remembered today on their own account, but they seem to have contributed something to the modern pantomime and variety show.

High burlesque prevails in all the plays I have considered in any detail; these are, or enclose, mock-plays, in which parody is sometimes more, sometimes less, prominent. Low burlesque also occurs from time to time, however: in the rivalry of the two Kings of Brentford, for instance.

My final words must constitute a reminder of the limited utility of the categories I have been employing. To distinguish theoretically between the various species of burlesque is a step towards clear thought on the subject; but, if we maintain that we can neatly separate all the particular literary phenomena with which we have been concerned into a limited number of sharply defined categories, we must be either deluding ourselves or distorting the phenomena for our own intellectual convenience. What we may legitimately assert is that all species of burlesque involve the use or the imitation of a serious subject-matter or style; that this use or imitation is so developed as to produce an incongruity between subject-matter and style; and that this incongruity provokes laughter. The word 'burlesque' derives from the Italian *burla*, 'ridicule'. While etymology cannot be allowed to dictate the meanings of the words we use, it does in this case draw our attention to what is central to the meaning of the word that interests us. Burlesque is mockery, it is joking, it is fun.

Select Bibliography

RICHMOND P. BOND's *English Burlesque Poetry 1700–1750* (Cambridge, Mass., 1932), though concerned solely with poetry during a single half-century, defines the species of burlesque in the way that I have followed in this more widely ranging study. While rarely attempting criticism, Bond supplies a useful historical narrative and a scholarly 'Register of Burlesque Poems'. GEORGE KITCHIN's *Survey of Burlesque and Parody in English* (Edinburgh, 1931) gives a general account of the subject, while dramatic burlesque receives special attention in V. V. R. G. C. CLINTON BADDELEY's *Burlesque Tradition in the English Theatre after 1660* (London, 1952).

Many of the poems discussed in the present book are readily available in the standard editions of their authors' works. Since the reader should have no difficulty in tracing them, I concentrate here upon the less accessible items. JOHN WILDERS' scholarly edition of SAMUEL BUTLER's *Hudibras* (Oxford, 1967) has an illuminating critical introduction and copious explanatory notes. DWIGHT MACDONALD's *Parodies: An Anthology from Chaucer to Beerbohm – and After* (London, 1961) contains many of the best parodies both in verse and in prose, including ten by Max Beerbohm. But more accurate texts of some of the earlier poems will be found in DAVID NICHOL SMITH's *Oxford Book of Eighteenth Century Verse* (Oxford, 1926), which includes also JONATHAN SWIFT's 'Baucis and Philemon' and an excerpt from JOHN GAY's *The Shepherd's Week*. Other useful anthologies are W. H. AUDEN's *Oxford Book of Light Verse* (Oxford, 1938), MICHAEL ROBERTS' *Faber Book of Comic Verse* (London, 1942), and the three volumes of 'Comic and Curious Verse' that J. M. COHEN has edited for Penguin Books. After a century of regular republication, HORACE and JAMES

SMITH's *Rejected Addresses* has gone out of print; but all good libraries have it, and second-hand copies are not yet scarce. CECIL DAY LEWIS' *An Italian Visit* (1953) is reprinted in his *Collected Poems* (London, 1954).

The best collection of parodies by MAX BEERBOHM is *A Christmas Garland* (London, 1912; new edition, 1950). HENRY FIELDING's *Joseph Andrews* and *Shamela* have been ably edited and annotated by DOUGLAS BROOKS in a single volume of the Oxford English Novels (London, 1970). STELLA GIBBONS' *Cold Comfort Farm* remains available as a paperback (Mayflower Books), and Penguin Books have published a paperback alternative to the standard edition of JAMES JOYCE's *Ulysses* (London, 1937).

CYRUS HOY edits *The Knight of the Burning Pestle* in volume i of *The Dramatic Works in the Beaumont and Fletcher Canon* (ed. Fredson Bowers, Cambridge, from 1966). There are also less elaborate editions of this play in the Regents Renaissance Drama Series, the Fountainwell Drama Texts, and the New Mermaid Series. To MONTAGUE SUMMERS we owe an interesting edition of BUCKINGHAM's *The Rehearsal* (Stratford-upon-Avon, 1914). HENRY FIELDING's *The Tragedy of Tragedies; or, The Life and Death of Tom Thumb the Great* has been fully edited by JAMES T. HILLHOUSE (New Haven, 1918), and more sparely in the Fountainwell Drama Texts. C. J. L. PRICE is re-editing the plays of R. B. SHERIDAN for the Clarendon Press, Oxford. In the meantime *The Critic* is conveniently available in the reprints of the plays included in the World's Classics and other series. HENRY CAREY's *Chrononhotonthologos*, after having been out of print for very many years, can now be obtained in SIMON TRUSSLER's *Burlesque Plays of the Eighteenth Century* (Oxford Paperbacks, 1969). This very useful volume contains also BUCKINGHAM's *The Rehearsal*, the 1730 version of FIELDING's *Tom Thumb*, *The Rovers* by GEORGE CANNING, J. H. FRERE, and GEORGE ELLIS, and six other plays.

Index